MW01225638

The Golden Years Become the Twilight Zone

(What to Expect, How to Prepare)

By Ron and Desiree Irvine

xulon
PRESS

Preface

We have worked with senior adults in our Adult Family Home for over six years. We have seen what they go through over the years running the home. This book will help you and tell you what to look for and help you to lighten your load with your loved ones. We will give you some ideas to help you get through these years.

I have also worked with mentally challenged people within a state run facility, and as a couple, my wife and I have worked with a group of girls in a run away home. Along with this, we have worked at churches within the youth and children ministries. We both have worked serving people for over thirty years.

I have a Bachelor of Arts degree in Biblical Studies, and a minor in Psychology and Physical Education. I also have a Master of Arts in Christian Counseling. I remember the saying "Life is tough, and it's tougher if you're stupid." That is true, but you know life is just tough, and you don't have to be stupid. It's just tough. Life can be easy, but is often times hard. You have the choice on how and what you make of it. It is your decision, so live life to it's fullest with no regrets. If you have Jesus Christ in your life, it will never end.

Contents

This book is dedicated to the sweet memory of Marie Smith, Ruth and Willis Irvine, and to the clients who passed away in our care. It is also dedicated to caregivers throughout the world who have given a part of their life to the service of the elderly.

CHAPTER ONE

When Do They Need Help?

May Sarton said "One thing is certain,
and I have always known it –
the joys of my life have nothing to do with age."

Recall how your parents raised you as a small child. There are always exceptions to the rule, but for the most part, I hope you felt the norm. They knew everything, were your protector, and all powerful. You didn't mind this. In fact, it gave you security along with love. Teenage years may have brought a few changes in your outlook, but hopefully there was a return of affection for them. As they go on to their retired years, you wish them happiness and fulfillment.

How is your outlook on growing older? What is your experience with age? Getting more information on aging can only help you in this journey. You will have the opportunity to follow along in the experiences I have had as an owner/worker of an adult family home. There will be much you can learn to help the elders you know, for you to consider, and also much information given to help you to plan ahead for your future, for their future.

From Nancy L. Mace, M.A. and Peter V. Rabins, M.D. in "THE 36 HOUR DAY", it is shared "in middle age many people start to notice that their memory seems to be slipping a bit. This is particularly true when they are tired or under stress. Naturally, they get worried that more serious troubles lie ahead. ... The large majority of healthy older people can expect some changes in memory function, not limiting, but troubling to the individual experiencing them. ... But all the evidence indicates that if an older person takes the time to learn something well, he or she will remember it as accurately as someone many decades younger. Thus, although older people think they are forgetting things more easily, in fact, what is happening is that they are not learning them as well in the first place."

Everyone ages in their own distinct way. Although many women dread it, aging is a normal process. We look upon it as years, but aging is also physical and mental. Everyone is different, so growing old is unique and individual for each person. According to research, it is age 75 when cells show normal aging changes. Yet, it is hard to rate a specific age because of the differences everyone has. Aging definitely happens, but it is influenced by heredity, life activities, stress, disease, and emotional allotment. Even though studies try to make groupings of certain aspects in aging, that is why it is so individual.

Dementia is a loss of touch or contact with reality, loss of mind or reasoning. It is organic and nonreversible. Some reasons for dementia are infection, dehydration causing poor nutrition, mineral imbalance, having your diabetes out of control, thyroid problems, tumors, medications, alcohol, small strokes, blood pressure problems, depression, and falls causing head injury. Reversible dementia can go away as situations change. Some of the problems just listed may be able to be taken care of, thus the dementia will leave.

From "2001 Current Medical Diagnosis and Treatment", written by Lawrence M. Tierney, Jr., Stephen J. McPhee and Maxine A. Papadakis the following is learned. "Older individuals experience occasional difficulty retrieving items from memory (usually manifested as word-finding complaints) and experiencing a slowing in their rate of information processing. By contrast, dementia is an acquired persistent and progressive impairment in intellectual function, with compromise in multiple cognitive domains at least one of which is memory. The demented patient's eficits must represent a significant decline in function and must be even enough to interfere with work or social life.

'Intellectual impairments in older patients are frequently the result of two other syndromes, each of which frequently coexists with dementia: depression and delirium. Depression is a common concomitant of dementia, but it can also masquerade as dementia. Moreover, a patient with depression and cognitive impairment whose intellectual function improves with treatment of the mood disorder has an almost fivefold greater risk of suffering irreversible dementia later in life. Delirium, characterized by acute confusion, occurs more commonly in patients with underlying dementia."

You can do exercises to keep your brain young. Learn to concentrate better by turning off the radio or television if you are trying to learn something new so you can concentrate better. Repeat what you want to remember. Make a mental picture. Adopt tried and true strategies to remember. If you have time, physically write down what you want to remember at least three times, maybe more. Exercise every day. A little bit of exercise goes a long way. Exercise can help your brain work better. There are these known facts to stay younger, but some people are still affected by different dementias.

Last week when you visited your parents or grandparents, you may have noticed a few concerns. In a waste basket, you noticed an unopened bill thrown away in error, while bright advertisement was on the kitchen table to look at. You helped your father find his misplaced glasses that were in the drawer in plain sight. You hide your disappointment when your parents seem more interested in their cat than their grandchildren you brought over. They keep singing the same song - one popular in the 50's. They mix up past happy times with the present, or are always recalling better times. Were they really better, or just a sweet memory of the past that has become sweeter with time? They often have a denial of their limitations that is frightening sometimes.

Scientists have tried many times to discover ways to solve the dementia problem, just as they have for cancer, Aids, and many other diseases. Hopefully, the answers will come soon although they are proving to be elusive for scientists at this point in time. From the book "Tangled Minds", by Muriel R. Gillick, M. D., dementia has been called "the disease of the century, the worst of all diseases. It is a collection of disorders producing progressing cognitive loss in multiple domains, including memory, language, and the capacity to solve the problems of daily life. Dementia affects four million Americans: 5 percent of those over sixty-five, but nearly 50 percent of those over eighty-five. The most common type is Alzheimer's disease, accounting for 60 to 70 percent of all cases. This translates into 2.5 million cases in the United States, and over 22 million cases worldwide. Because it is so common, dementia will touch the lives of us all. Even if we ourselves escape, our spouses or our friends or our parents will be affected."

That being the case, we all need to be aware of dementia characteristics so we can try and be ahead of it; be forewarned. Answering difficult questions is a part of this. If dementia does come upon you, what do you want to happen? Who do you want to take care of you? Where do you want to live? How do you want to live? Instead of answering pat answers that do not really give a solution, search out the area you live in to find out what it offers. Ask your spouse, children, and parents these questions so if a need for answers comes upon any of you, you will know you are respecting their desires. Express your feelings so your desires will be followed also.

Have a check up with your doctor if your memory changes, even if you don't want to admit it to anyone. For two or three years someone may be aware their memory is not as good as it had been. First, they have trouble remembering dates and names. When they write things down to remember it helps, but they get frustrated when they are constantly searching for a word to use in conversation.

Oftentimes, dementias will start out this way, and no one realizes it until later when another illness comes upon the patient. Frequently, the suffering will deny their problems. This is not only because they may be private or resistant to care, but because they are truly sick and cannot honestly tell you what is wrong, even though they are aware of life being a little different. It may be so different they are afraid of it and think it will go away if ignored.

The suffering will often argue with you adamantly when you try and place them elsewhere to live for their own best interests. This is not because they like to argue, but simply because they are unable to be completely aware of their situation. They are used to life that way, even if it is more troublesome, because change is hard. If they move, they may complain they won't know anyone.

You can tell them they will meet new people. They say they have met enough people. You can tell them there are people to help them. They may say they don't need any help, even if they are aware they do need help. Their feelings are very mixed up, along with their mind, so they can no longer understand completely, or reason well with you. Continue on with them, even when it is frustrating, because they definitely need you to be a part of their life. Even if it is your decision to take them out of their home, against their wishes, it may be the best decision you make for them, as they are led off kicking and screaming. Stay strong, because the overall need is for them to have safety. This is hard for many children because they are now being forced to play the parental force for their own parents. Realize you are not alone. This is a new problem and with health becoming better, more people are staying alive longer, so this is a new difficulty and hardship for many people. It is just awkward to admit this to yourself, your friends, your family. But this concern has come up for you and your loved ones. You want the best care for them. Can you do this alone, or do you need help? The best first step is to find out as much as you can about it.

Generally speaking, there are unique characteristics that follow all elderly. From Marianne Shneider Corey and Gerald Corey, in their book "Groups Process and Practice", they shared the following points:

"1. The attention span of some elderly people may be short because of physical or psychological difficulties. ...

2. The elderly often are taking medications that interfere with their ability to be fully present.

3. With some who are in advanced stages of senility, reality orientation becomes a problem. ...

4. Regular attendance of meetings can be problematic because of physical ailments, transportation problems, interruptions in the schedules of institutions, and conflicting appointments with doctors, social workers, and other professionals.

5. Older people often need support and encouragement more than they need confrontation. ...

6. The elderly have a great need to be listened to and understood. Respect is shown by accepting them through hearing their underlying messages and not treating them in a condescending way. The elderly often suffer from "conversation deprivation." To be encouraged to share and relate with others has therapeutic value in itself (Burnside, 1984).

7. Some people are more difficult to reach. ...

8. Themes more prevalent with the elderly than with other age groups include loss; loneliness and social isolation; poverty; feelings of rejection; the struggle to find meaning in life; dependency; feelings of uselessness, hopelessness, and despair; fears of death and dying; grief over other's deaths; sadness over physical and mental deterioration; and regrets over past events.

9. Loss is probably the central theme of growing old. Anxiety, low self esteem, and somatic complaints are typical responses to the losses faced by elderly persons (Hern & Weis, 1991). We live most of our adult years with an internal focus of control. As we age, we have to adjust to an increasingly external focus of control when confronted with losses over which we have little control. Physical disabilities and sensory impairments contribute to the social isolation experienced by very old people (Myers, 1990).

10. Normal aging does not necessarily equate with illness and frailty. Chronic diseases and disabilities increase with age, but as Hazzard, Larson, and Perls (1998) point out, disease and disability can be deterred or mitigated with interventions such as proper nutrition and exercise. ... The quality of life of our elders can be improved by encouraging them to increase their functional abilities."

Now is the time to learn about dementia. What in the world is it, and how does it affect me, and others? There are seven levels of dementia in the Global Deterioration Scale for Assessment of **Primary Degenerative Dementia**. They are:

1. Alzheimer's,
2. Multi Infarct Dementia (meaning an actual part of the brain has died),
3. Parkinsonian type (epidemiology tremors and rigidity),
4. Picks disease,
5. Cruetzfeldt-Jakcb disease,
6. AIDS,
7. Korsakoff's disease (long term alcohol use).

Differences from cortical dementia and primary degenerative dementia are listed in Harriet Hodgson's book "Alzheimer's, Finding The Words, A Communication Guide For Those Who Care". She lists three types of **cortical dementia**: (cortical dementia pertains to actions or conditions of the cerebral cortex. This has to do with the brain and intellect.)

"(1) primary degenerative dementia (eg, Alzheimer's) accounting for about 50-60% of cases;

(2) atherosclerotioc (multi-infarct) dementia, 15-20% of cases (this figure is probably low because of the tendency to overuse the diagnosis of Alzheimer's dementia);

(3) mixtures of the first two types of dementia due to miscellaneous causes, 15-20% of cases.

Examples of **primary degenerative dementia** are Alzheimer's dementia (most common) and Pick, Creutzfeldt-Jakob, and Huntington dementias (less common). Alzheimer's disease strikes the most people suffering dementia. Yet it is important to know about all of the dementias to get a full picture of the total problems."

Information regarding **atherosclerotioc (multi infarct) dementia** is found in "Alzheimers, Finding The Words, A Communication For Those Who Care", by Harriet Hodgson also stated that "the mental impairment of multi-infarct dementia (MID) occurs as a result of cerebral vascular disease and small strokes throughout the brain. The likelihood of this disease increases with hypertension and diabetes, which are risk factors for strokes. It features a step-like deterioration of thinking functions and an abnormal neurologic examination. These individuals often have abnormal gait and strength in association with their dementia. It's progression is different than Alzheimer's disease in that with each descending step there may be abrupt worsening, and between episodes there may be mild improvement.'

'The progression of the disease may be somewhat arrested if the risk factors which predispose the patient to stroke are treated effectively. These factors are similar to those for heart disease: hypertension, diabetes, obesity, high cholesterol, smoking, and heart disease.

Parkinsonism is a disease originating in an abnormality of brain function in which, for the most part, the mind remains unaffected also. However, in the degenerative hardening of the arteries of the brain or in cerebrovascular stroke, both brain physiology and mind physiology are intimately involved."

Unfortunately, people with this disease do not have many options to change their fate. Like cancer, there is much research being done on Parkinson's to help alter the destiny of many sufferers. Yet, at the present moment, no answer is imminent in the search for ways to stop it. It is interesting how each dementia follows it's own specific rules. This is seen further in Parkinson's disease. From "The 36 Hour Day", Nancy L. Mace, M.A., and Peter V. Rabins, M.D., M.P.H. share the following regarding this disease. "Parkinsonism is a mild or severe disorder of the body movement characterized by slow mobility, stiffness, and tremor; also known as Parkinson's disease. Most of the million and a half victims of the disorder are over 60. ... True parkinsonism is a disorder of a particular group of brain cells that normally release a substance called dopamine which is essential to the regulation of normal body movement."

Another type of primary degenerative dementia is Creutzfeldt-Jakob disease. "Thoughts From Wolfelt" by Alan D. Batesville Management Services share more on this disease. "Creutzfeldt Jakob disease is transmissible in brain or eye tissue to primates, including humans. ...'Creutzfeldt Jakob disease presents itself usually in late middle age with rapidly progressive dementia, myoclomic fasciculations, ataxia, and somnolence and has an electroencephalographic pattern characterized by paroxysms with high voltages and slow waves. The four forms of Creutzfeld Jakob disease are sporadic (80-85%), familial (15%), iatrogenic (< 1%), and a new variant (also rare)... 'There is a rapid decline to akinetic mutism. There are no definitive risk factors for Creutzfeldt Jakob disease."

Can you recall your high school health teacher and what they told you about eating? To keep healthy, you need to be active physically and mentally, and <u>eat properly.</u> You may cringe and shudder at this reminder, but it is true. Try it and see. The results will really improve your health and outlook on life. In "Life After Loss" Raymond Moody Jr. and Diane Arcangel share the importance of vitamin B. "A deficiency of vitamin B1 leads to neurological disorders, especially to the psychosis known as Korsakoff's syndrome, characterized by memory impairment and time and place disorientation, to paralysis of the extremities (beriberi) and to heart failure. People who eat substandard diets and those whose food is overcooked (thiamin is destroyed by heat) may not be getting enough B1 in their food. Signs of deficiency can be detected by a doctor and corrected with a prescribed regimen of thiamin."

One of the newest dementias that has developed in recent years is AIDs. AIDs dementia is usually always also connected to health choices. Nancy L. Mace, M.A. and Peter V. Rabins, M. D., M. P. M., in "The 36 Hour Day" share this information also. "AIDs dementia complex (HIV associated cognitive/motor complex) is the most common cause of mental status changes in HIV infected patients. The diagnosis is one of exclusion based on a brain imaging study and spinal fluid analysis that exclude other pathogens. Neuropsychiatric testing is helpful in distinguishing patients with dementia from those with depression. Patients with AIDS dementia complex typically have difficulty with cognitive tasks and exhibit diminished motor speed. Patients may first notice a deterioration in their handwriting. The manifestations of dementia may wax and wane, with persons exhibiting periods of lucidity and confusion over the course of a day. Although the mechanism by which HIV causes neurologic dysfunction is not completely understood, many patients improve with effective antiretroviral treatment."

Many avenues are being researched to understand the disease of Alzheimer's more and stop it. "The 36-Hour Day" by N. L. Mace and P.V. Rabins shares about this more. "Alzheimer's disease is a progressive brain disorder in which the nerve cells degenerate and the size of the brain shrinks, resulting in dementia - a deterioration in mental functioning. Alzheimer's disease is the cause of more than 75 percent of documented cases of dementia in North Americans over sixty-five years of age."

There are four distinct facets of dementia in **Alzheimer's**. They start out with minimal annoyances that go into life taking adversities. Following are specific troubles people bothered with dementia will encounter: (They may not be bothered by many of these troubles at first, or they may be bothered very much by all of them listed. Every case is individual.)

Point 1: (FORGETFUL) (DISORGANIZED) (Levels 1 and 2)

forgetful For the suffering, it is easy to forget names, happy memories, phone numbers, get lost in accustomed surroundings, have difficulty telling time, have troubles in making decisions or coming to a conclusion, become easily angered, irritable, and aware of losses.

In **Level 1** there is no complaint of forgetfulness, or memory loss. There is no cognitive decline. No apparent memory decline in doctor checks is seen, yet the process has begun..

In **Level 2** mild forgetfulness appears. A woman may complain about forgetting where she put her purse, her husband will complain about trying to find his wallet. They start to forget names of friends.

In **Level 2** there is mild related decline shown by forgetfulness. It will occur where one has placed familiar objects or forgetting names of people one knows well. Appointments may be forgotten easily at this time also.

Point 2: (LATE CONFUSION - EARLY DEMENTIA) (Levels 3 and 4)

In **Level 3**, observers will notice early confusion coming upon the suffering person. It is not until the severity of these losses is seen that the term dementia is used. This stage shows the earliest of clear-cut deficiencies. The patient may get lost easily. Co-workers can see poor performance that did not used to be a part of the patient's work habits. Clients have trouble with the word-finding problems. It is hard for the patient to remember words and names. A patient can read a newspaper or book, but only retain portions of what they read. It is also easy for them to misplace an object of value.

They return to earlier language, have difficulty following the story line, making plans, and problem solving. They forget the normal every day routine, cleanliness habits taught in childhood, lose items easily and claim they are stolen. Often, one troubled this way will have no idea of reality or what is truly going on. They will complain of imagined neglect, are easily in a bewildered state, have smaller attention spans, and often refuse help with ADL's (activities of daily living) using an angry manner to try and stop others from helping them. They have a curtailed ability to do their finances, and have extreme anxiety often on small matters. (Will I have enough money for milk if I splurge on ice cream?) They often use denial to cope, and can be very restless and impatient. Their social skills may still be there at this time. The patient usually adamantly denies every problem they are going through at this time. Some anxiety is associated with these symptoms. With all of the changes going on, that is almost an understatement. Yet everyone handles these changes in unique ways. So many people are different on how they accept the changes in their life. There are definite deficits in occupational and social settings in Level 3.

In **Level 4** late confusion is evident. There is a definite loss of memory shown with clinical interviews. The loss is mainly seen in the following ways: loss of knowledge of current and/or recent events, they may not be able to recall all of their history, they have a decreased talent on handling their finances and their ability to travel is harder. They start to have no desire or be unable to do complex tasks. Denial has become very much a part of their everyday life.

Point 3: EARLY TO MIDDLE DEMENTIA, SEVERE MENTAL LOSS (Levels 5 and 6)

For **Level 5** there is a moderately severe loss which brings us to the early stages of actual dementia. Many changes come upon the one suffering. Their gait changes. Sufferers use small steps, halting often, and have increased rigidity. They also have an intolerance to cold, in addition to bowel and bladder incontinence. They decrease in their ability to read, and do math (dysgraphia, dyscalculi). Additionally, they have a lessened ability to understand and express language (aphasia). That is why it is important to make sure they understand what you are saying, before going on to more detailed conversation. Their ability in purposeful movement (apraxia) is lessened, and they have a decreased ability to recognize objects (agnosia). Often times, they will persevere against those in leadership roles, and wander off, getting lost easily. Many become immodest causing much embarrassment for observers, although they are not aware of this at all.

Others suffering from Alzheimer's begin to have swallowing problems, needing help in their eating. Additionally, some sufferers are affected with paranoia, agitation, hallucinations and delusions, and/or violent behavior. Just like the knowledge that everyone is different is apparent to everyone, reactions to dementia are different for many, although there are many commonalities.

In **Level 5** there is the beginning of severe decline and patients move into "early dementia." The person can't survive without help. There is often some disorientation to place and/or time. They can no longer remember any history of their life, e. g., telephone number, name of the school they went to. Yet, incredibly, they still remember many aspects of their life. They may not need help dressing or eating, but assistance for the choice of clothes is often essential. They wear the trappings of a healthy person and are all dressed up with nowhere to go. They are relatively good in social skills and language. They believe they still have responsibilities and do not need any help to do them, although they do. Their perception of truth and reality are based upon errors with their thinking. At this point, they are still able to form a thought, and carry through to accomplish it. They deny they need assistance, yet their understanding of certainty and facts in life is based on misunderstandings.

The person in **Level 5** still has the ability to think, plan an action, and do it. Yet their behaviors are sometimes normal and sometimes not. They start to wander even more, forgetting where they were going. It's hard for someone not troubled with this disease to fully understand them. They forget where they are going because they are no longer able to keep hold of their thoughts in a consistent manner. They go out to the yard, but don't remember they were going to go to the mailbox, or possibly into the car you have just started up for them. It is easier for them when they get to certain points of the disease for you to just give them simple one step directions. When they get that direction accomplished, go on to the next one.

They start to have delusions more with suspicious and anxious thoughts regarding their loss of short term memory. They frequently become tearful and depressed. The transition into Level 6 is often difficult. The environment often sparks behavior, but they are still often resistant to caregiving help. They need supervision in eating, toileting, bathing, dressing, and grooming. They often have sleep disturbances and fear being left alone. They socially interact well with people in Level 6, but not Level 7. They may still have sexual drives and desires.

In **Level 6** there is severe mental capacity and the patient moves into "middle dementia". At this time, they will often forget the name of their spouse or main helper. They become largely unaware of all recent events and experiences in their lives. They may have a few memories, but it is all lacking, and incomplete. They are often not aware of the season, year, or where they are at. They have trouble counting from 1 to 10 or 10 to 1. They need help with all of their daily activities and are often incontinent. They can usually remember their name. This is the time when their personality changes and many alterations occur. These changes are different for everyone, but include 1) delusional actions, 2) obsessive symptoms, 3) anxiety symptoms, agitation, and some violent behavior may occur, 4) the loss of fortitude and moral fiber. They can no longer hold a thought long enough to figure out what the next step should be.

Point 4: LATE DEMENTIA (Level 7)

When they get to **Level 7**, they are in the last stages of life. This is late dementia, where they are "in their own world". They have lost their social graces and wear clothing inappropriately. They often seem lost in thought and it is hard for them to keep attention.

They have a great deal of trouble recognizing common objects and they have the beginning of downward restricted gaze; loss of 3-D vision. They need total assistance in all aspects of life.In Level 7 there are seizures, myoclonic jerking, slowed movements, lip smacking, and severe loss of body weight. There is also little response to stimuli given to them and indifference to food. It is often hard to get them excited about food at all, and they often need to be fed food that is of baby food subsistence. They have forgotten how to chew, and need to be told how to do this. Additional help with swallowing is also needed. At this time, you can stroke their neck to help them swallow correctly. There is also a loss of verbal competency and understanding , and they often times use agitation to communicate.

Verbal abilities are gone. Frequently there is no talking - just grunts. The person at this time needs complete help in eating and toileting. They loose their ability to walk. The brain is no longer able to tell the body what to do. They wear their clothing inappropriately, often taking off and putting on socks and shoes. They are uncomfortable wearing any additional dress, and many times don't wear their supportive appliances. They no longer have any social graces and it is very hard for them to speak because they cannot find the words they want. Then it is all uphill work for them to comprehend what you are trying to convey. It is laborious work to keep their attention because they are often lost in thought. They have specific troubles also with their body in posture, gait and balance. They have a hard time sitting up properly, and holding up their head, in addition to the swallowing problems mentioned. Their physical abilities are much like a new born baby. They also have a complete loss of 3-D vision at this time.

They may keep some overlearned skills from the past and frequently their senses are heightened. Their wandering pattern is very sensory oriented, but they no longer recognize relatives or people taking care of them. They may sometimes have huge verbal outbursts because of their inability to understand and communicate. They can no longer properly communicate requirements they have. They need total care in their eating, toileting, bathing, dressing, and grooming. They will accept someone speaking to them, but usually will not start the interaction themselves.

From "Life After Loss" by Raymond Moody Jr. and Dianne Arcangel further information regarding Alzheimer's can be learned. "Possible risk factors for Alzheimer's Disease are: female gender, small strokes or cerebrovascular disease, Parkinson's disease, race and ethnicity, environmental toxins, diet, lack of exercise, stress, depression before onset of Alzheimer's disease. Additional research is needed to clarify their role, since studies about these possible factors have not been thoroughly carried out. There is considerable speculation over how much or how little these factors influence the development of Alzheimer's disease. Nevertheless, identifying and changing just one of these factors that could be modified to reduce the risk of developing Alzheimer's would have enormous implications. For example, if it were known for certain that a particular food or chemical increased the risk of developing the disease, such things could be avoided and the number of people with Alzheimer's disease could be substantially reduced."

The reason why one possible risk factor is women is because Alzheimer's disease is associated with old age, and women usually outlive men. To avoid strokes, we should keep our blood pressure down and avoid smoking.

Furthermore, it was stated in the same book "Life After Loss" by Raymond Moody, Jr. and Dianne Arcangel the ties between Alzheimer's and Parkinson's disease. "Another medical condition that appears to pose a risk for developing Alzheimer's is Parkinson's disease, a neurological disorder that impairs the movement of hands, arms, and legs. Between 20 and 30 percent of people with Parkinson's disease develop symptoms of Alzheimer's disease, typically in the last stages of the disease. Likewise, most people in the late stages develop some symptoms of Parkinson's disease. The relationship between these two brain diseases is not yet fully understood."

As caregivers and/or power of attorneys, we need to remember the patients are not who they were earlier in life, and to stop trying to get them to remember when. The hardest thing to learn is that which was important to these clients isn't what they recall. They can't remember - but what they experience with you moment by moment. When they act differently, don't act like their child and be hurt. You can't act like their children, afraid you can't please them, but act as if they were someone not related to you. You have to jump out of the behavior patterns you have had for years, and realize you can't change their behavior. Remember they are not totally aware of everything. Let them live at their own speed, and be content. They live with Alzheimer's and accept it better than a lot of family and friends. In the later stages of Alzheimer's, they are quite content.

In one study, it was shown that African Americans had four times the risk and in another study, five times the risk for developing Alzheimer's disease compared to other races, no matter what their educational levels were. Another large study showed higher rates of Alzheimer's for Japanese who emigrated to Hawaii compared to those who remained in Japan. Other studies revealed a very low percentage of Alzheimer's in Cherokee Indians in Oklahoma. Until more solid information is discovered, it is a guessing game. It is depressing for many, but much work is being done to help control and stop this disease.

Many studies have been done on possible environmental triggers such as aluminum, mercury, zinc, and iron, but so far no environmental toxin has been discovered to cause Alzheimer's. The role of diet as a cause for Alzheimer's is just now being investigated. The affects of lack of exercise are not conclusive. It is good for the body physically to exercise and that does stop or slow down some diseases, but no conclusive evidence has come about regarding Alzheimer's disease. Other studies pertaining to stress and Alzheimer's disease are also inconclusive at this time.

Another risk factor for Alzheimer's Disease is depression before the onset of Alzheimer's. There is evidence that some people with Alzheimer's have shown depressive symptoms before they came down with Alzheimer's. They may complain of loss of energy, loss of interest, or feeling different. When tested, there are no results regarding Alzheimer's. It isn't until many years later they show definite symptoms. It is hard to know if depression truly plays a role yet as a cause.

From David Kuhn's book "Alzheimer's, Early Stages" important points can be listed. "Alzheimer's disease has 9 crucial symptoms. ...

1. Recent memory loss (computer skills, running household, etc.)
2. Difficulty with familiar tasks (such as dressing, cooking, and driving)
3. Speech problems (telling the same stories over and over again, drifting off during conversation)
4. Time and place mix-ups (like Mom going to the morning church service at night)poor judgment (leaving doors unlocked, standing nude in front of windows, not wearing a coat in winter, etc.)
5. Trouble with abstract thinking (difficulty with cause and effect reasoning, inability to understand analogies)
6. Misplacing or losing things (including the tendency to squirrel things away in odd places)
7. Changes in mood and behavior (treating loved ones like strangers)
8. Personality changes (emotional outbursts, quickly shifting from gentle to hostile, etc.)
9. Loss of motivation (generally passive behavior and the constant desire to sleep)

If I have any advice for caregivers, it's trust your instincts - those inner messages that tell you something is wrong."

A person with dementia is usually good with habitual skills that require no active thinking. Their primary motor functions to begin with are very good at the first stages, depending on whether there are additional health troubles or not. For the most part, their strength is still there, plus good dexterity and motor control. Yet directions broken down into simple steps are needed to give them help in starting and stopping. They can still experience sensations, good or bad. Their emotions are also very active, so they need outlets for them. Their sense of rhythm will stay along with their sense of movement. Because of this, they can still often enjoy music, dancing , sanding, threading, folding, rocking and swinging. In nice weather, get them out in your large swing if you have one. They can visit and swing to their hearts content, and really enjoy the fresh air.

David Kuhn, M. S. W., in his book, "Alzheimer's, Early Stages" draws new information from scientists. "Just as scientists seem to be drawing together the disparate strands of Alzheimer's research, new observations are coming to light that may radically alter our understanding of the disease. Atherosclerosis, long discounted as a cause of dementia, is now recognized both as the cause of a subtype of dementia (multi infarct dementia) and, even more surprising, as a modulating factor in Alzheimer's disease: patients with pathologic signs of Alzheimer's turn out to be far more demented if they have strokes as well. Plaques and tangles, believed to be the defining characteristics of Alzheimer's disease, have recently been joined by a third, previously unrecognized brain lesion. Just as Alois Alzheimer identified neurofibrillary tangles using a special staining technique, researchers today found the new plaque like lesions with an innovative labeling technique."

Near the end, the ill may accept, but not initiate interaction There is a lot of resistance to caregiving in all of their tasks of daily living. They have a hard time communicating their needs. Their speech is limited to about six words a day. Vocabulary responses from them will only be in singular words, not phrases or sentences. Frequently, all verbal response is lost - only grunting. They loose their ability to walk. They are no longer able to sit up or hold their head up, and the ability to smile is lost. The brain becomes so weak, it is unable to tell the body what to do.

There are real physical concerns they may have: stroke, diabetes, cancer, bad hearts, etc. There are also many mental illnesses that may affect them. You know they need help, even if it is refused, but what should your next step be?

CHAPTER TWO

How to Take Care of Your Loved Ones

Failing to plan is planning to fail.
–Anonymous

When you notice your parents or other loved elders changing into people that do need help, there are some actions you can take. Decide if they need physical, or emotional help. Is it both? Are you in denial of their needs? As their child or spouse, it is often hard to distance yourself enough to make an informed judgment. When they go to the doctor the next time, go with them. If they're not happy with this, simply make up a good excuse. Even if they are beginning to have troubles, they often desire to still be completely in control of their life. Smile, think up a good whatfor, and tag along. Pick up as much information as possible so you can know the complete situation. If you are power of attorney, you need to know information to relate to the rest of the family.

Some of your concerns may just be part of the normal aging process. Physical changes in the aging process will be cardiac and respiratory troubles. They may be having problems with their mouth, teeth, and digestion. This is because as you grow older, your tissues shrink. Do they have osteoporosis? Weight bearing exercises help with this. If this is the case, set up a program for them to help with strengthening them more. Our skin, hair, fingernails, and toenails also change as our skin becomes thinner and dryer. Their skin may actually tear very easily.

Sometimes, when people age, they don't pick up their feet as easily when walking. For this reason, scatter rugs are not a good idea in homes where they live. Do their vision, hearing, taste and smell still work just as well, or are they declining in these abilities? Change the home they live in as much as possible to accommodate their new needs. How are their neurological and immune systems? Do they hurt when you touch them? When they become older, their process of perception often lessons. What types of food do they like to eat? Are there any allergies caused from food they eat or because of where they live?

If they have been moved to a home that gives care, these next caregiving supports should automatically be done by staff. If not, find another place that will care for them properly. If they are still living alone, you may be the only person caring for them. If they need help with transfers from a wheelchair or chair, stand close to them with a broad base of support. Encourage them to lean against you if needed. Assist them at the waist by grasping their belt for firmer support and hold their hand firmly. Bend your knees and hips, keeping your back straight. Get as close to them as possible, and move in the direction of the transfer. It's important to remember this so you won't hurt yourself in transfers. When helping to transfer people remember the rhyme, 'nose over toes'. Stand on their weaker side. Walk at their pace synchronizing your steps with them.

These patients may often need help going up and down stairs. If they need to go up and down often, and are unsafe with their mobility, you should consider installing a stairlift. When walking upstairs, stand two steps below the person. Ask them to hold onto the banister, and keep them steady by putting one hand on each hip. Walk up slowly. For going downstairs, stand two steps below the person, facing them. Place your hands on their hips and walk down slowly. For better balance, keep both feet on the same step. All of these safety hints help to have a smoother care set up which helps them to remain happy and calmer as the days go by.

Psychological events occurring in the aging process can be

considered stress points also. How do they relate with their family, finances, work, effects of stress and loss, and their abilities to accept grief, depression, and anxiety? These are heavy considerations for all ages, and become harder to be able to do and accept when you age.

Main considerations that you, the power of attorney, or family members need to consider and be in agreement about are:

1. **Addressing legal and financial affairs**. Have a Power of Attorney appointed. This may be hard for some families, but is essential to help make the unforeseen future smoother and easier for everyone. Families should think of the future. Death is a hard part of life to accept, but it happens; to all of us. No one knows when their time on earth will be finished, so it is best to plan ahead for the rest of the family to be provided for. Having a Power of Attorney to help when problems come about will shift the decisions off of the ill person onto the family advocate that will help carry on with the decisions made by the ill person when they were well.

2. **Rethinking the living situation**. Is the loved one safe living alone? Independence is a point to consider, but so is the safety of a sick person. Can they safely dress, fix their own meals, clean, carry on with no help? What type of living arrangement would be best for them now? Consider and check out all options; living alone, adult day services, adult family homes, board & care homes, assisted living, nursing homes, and psychiatric hospitals.

3. **Choosing a physician and other professionals.** Depending on the needs of the elderly, try and find a doctor for them that deals in these needs. You'll be farther ahead in the game of helping them so much more quickly if you are working with a doctor that has the correct information and solutions you need.

4. **Explore community resources**. Contact senior centers, schools, state resources, community centers, and churches for information on places that will help you in your desire to find help. They will often have many good suggestions because people feel comfortable in these situations and talk easily of their concerns.

5. **Learn more about the debilitating disease.** The only way you can be more insightful and guided correctly on the path you should take for yourself and your loved one is to get as much

information as you can regarding the specific trouble they have. Keep abreast with new ideas regarding the disease so you can ask the doctor if these new possibilities you've read about would help.

Everyone affected by dementia has concerns and hardships as they try to continue on in life. This is seen in many of these illnesses, especially Alzheimer's. Daniel Kuhn, from "Alzheimer's Early Stages" shares more on this. "Since the person with Alzheimer's Disease no longer possesses the mental skills to be completely independent, a special brand of leadership is called for. At least one person must assume overall authority for ensuring the well-being of the person with Alzheimer's Disease but it is best to include others too if at all possible. Much work is involved in addressing basic physical needs like food and shelter as well as the psychological and social needs. ... You need not be afraid of taking this important leadership role or a major part of it, although it may feel awkward at first. The person with Alzheimer's Disease needs your help. If possible, it is best to share this role with someone else or at least to delegate some of the responsibilities to others who are willing to help and support your efforts."

If the suffering person is intent on making bad decisions there are three ways to change their direction. They need a change of circumstance. You can follow the physical alternative and use medication. If that is not desired, try massage. This gets them thinking of something else while they enjoy the feel of massage. Massage can be used or other activities they can do that they still enjoy. Some of these activities would be structured routines. They don't have to necessarily be anything that active. Just getting up at the same time every morning, having the same type of coffee or breakfast they like, listening to music they like, or watching a favorite TV show might get them on another train of thought and away from the bad choice idea. If they are able to walk, take them for a walk. Point out the homes around them to get them looking at different objects and thinking of something else.

Usually, they love companionship. Get a tape of music they like, play it, and show them physical exercises to do with it if they are still able to be active. If they are Christian, and/or like being read to, you can read verses to help encourage them. The following verses will do just that:

Psalms 23 to Psalms 34, Psalms 1, 5, 8, 42, 43, Psalms 145 to Psalms 150, Psalms 95 to Psalms 100, Psalms 16 to Psalms 19, Psalms 138 to Psalms 139, Romans 8, 12 and 13, I Corinthians 13, II Corinthians 4 to II Corinthians 6, Hebrews 11 to Hebrews 13, I John 1 to I John 3, Revelations 21 to Revelations 22. Use these, or other verses they especially like. Also, you can read their favorite hymns, songs, or poems to them. This all helps them feel like they are still a part of the family or group they live in instead of being stuck away to be forgotten.

Some environmental modifications can be done on the home so they can be safer still. Get door buzzers for at night to warn you/caregiver they have decided to wander. Put visual barriers up in the yard, or signs for them to see and help direct back, or exit alarms. Increased lighting is good for any yard and enclosed court-yards help them to stay in one area.

They have the right to make a choice. You just need to learn to reason with them and negotiate the risks. This can be trying for the caregiver, so pull yourself up and use the patience you have learned through life. Remember that the relative or client you work with is a different person now than in younger years. They did not purposely plan to be needing the help and direction they need now. They did not change into the person they are now to cause you trouble and sadness. Thus, the heavy word 'patience' needs to be used by all caregivers. Here are further cues to be aware of when the decision to move them has finally been reached. Determine the best way to take care of the loved one so you can give instructions to helpers, or other places where they may live. For example, what are their specific needs for bathing? How about the proper care of their fingernails, toenails, shaving? Do you know? What about eating needs? When moving a person, instruct the caregiver properly so the client will be taken care of safely and the way they are accus-tomed to. It isn't always possible to convey desires fully, but if it is, it helps workers in the adjustment period immensely. General knowledge is assumed by workers when you take the person need-ing help there, yet every peculiarity of the person is important for caregivers to know so they can help the client better in the specific way that is desired by that one person.

Observe the place you are visiting and considering. How does it look? Are they are interested in cleanliness? How does the home, clinic, retirement center, nursing home smell? Do you notice any gloves being worn? Has any worker washed their hands during your visit? It is important to try and find a place strong in guarding against infection. These are just a few ways to deduct if cleanliness is an important aspect for them or not. You have to determine the strengths and education of caregivers and their abilities, mannerisms, personalities, and training when the client has poor judgment, difficulty recognizing objects, wandering, forgetfulness, and the inability to solve problems. Ask where the medicine is kept to see if it is locked, or free for the sick person to take at any time. Freedom is an important aspect in life, but it should not be used regarding medicines if the client is unable to make right decisions using them. All medicines should be locked up.

From gathered information, you can decide what is needed for this new road in their life. Include siblings so there are no misunderstandings and you can draw wisdom, strength, and encouragement from one another. The saying two heads are better than one is true, when you are making such serious and emotional changes with loved ones. David Kuhn, in "Alzheimer's Early Stages" verifies this also. "It is important to involve others in planning, initiating, and executing these activities, since you will eventually need help. It is unrealistic and psychologically unhealthy for both you and your loved one with AD for you to be fully responsible for all activities at all times."

The suffering one can still watch you or others do activities even if they are unable to do the same thing anymore themselves. They can help you by making cookies, or simply observing, watching and listening, depending on their level of abilities. When they are involved, they can take enjoyment in helping others and being included. Although Alzheimer's and other mind debilitating diseases limit their abilities to do everything like before, they can often still reminisce and take part in spiritual and religious practices they are used to. Showing them your acceptance helps them feel valued. That is especially important for this segment of society - to show them honor and proper care.

If they are basically healthy, except for mind concerns, help them keep on a healthy diet. Exercises are often available at senior centers or health organizations (YMCA) for them. All of this helps to keep them healthier, although you may need to take part in accomplishing these events with them. How will they get there safely, etc.? Assist them as needed, whether it be in dressing, walking, transferring, eating.

At the beginning, you will wonder 'Where will I find the time?' Even when retired, this will take time. If you are still working, explore the benefits of the Family and Medical Leave Act. This Act requires employers with fifty or more employees to grant up to twelve weeks of unpaid leave a year for the care of a parent, spouse, or child with a serious health concern.

More care instructions were found in Daniel Kuhn's book, "Alzheimer's Early Stages". "The changing nature of the relationship between you and the person with Alzheimer's Disease will often be reflected in the variety of decisions that now need to be made. Several areas of concern, typically involving safety and well-being, come to the for in the early stages: driving a car, managing medications, maintaining a proper diet, and handling finances. The ability of people with Alzheimer's disease who live alone to remain independent becomes questionable and issues related to their personal freedom may come up. There may be a clash between the preferences of the person with Alzheimer's disease and your perceptions of his or her needs. You will need to be assertive in dealing with these practical matters, since the person with Alzheimer's Disease is not likely to initiate lifestyle changes without some direction. If you do not adopt a proactive stance, a crisis is likely to develop. In other words, if you do not act, you could eventually pay a heavy price."

One of the first topics to consider is having someone formally designated to act regarding legal and financial decisions. Many illnesses take away capacity for the patient to think clearly. Someone needs to become the Durable Power of Attorney (DPA). They become the patient's legal minder. Two types are available: one for health-care decisions and one for financial affairs. Living wills pertain only to end-of-life decisions, not all health decisions. Living trusts are legal decisions that require an attorney.

Final questions to consider before a move is made:

1. Can the loved one live alone without any help whatsoever?
2. Can the loved one live alone with some, medium, or total help? Decide need of help.
3. Decide where this help will come from. Family, neighbor, caregiver, visiting nurse, live in nurse? Can the person live safely with adult day services at their home? Does the person need to be moved to an assisted living situation, adult family home, nursing home, or psychiatric hospital?

If shots are needed, can the loved one administer them alone, or do they need help? A nurse must give the shots if needed, and if the patient cannot be taught how to properly give them. Depending on the level of help needed, choices can be made. Further information is taken from "Tangled Minds" by Muriel R. Gillick. "A person with a dementing illness is less able to take responsibility for his own safety. He is no longer able to evaluate consequences the way the rest of us do, and, because he forgets so quickly, accidents can easily happen." Go into educating yourself so you can be the best help for your loved one.

For different diseases, different menus are needed. This is especially true for diabetics, Parkinson, and heart disease patients. A good diet is also a must for depressed people and people with dementia. Drugs can cause nutritional deficiencies so it is important to find out from your doctor or pharmacist how the medicine will affect a person so it can be counteracted with other foods. If weight continues to be lost, a person should seek out a dietitian for an assessment and create a nutritional meal plan. Also, it is important to provide well balanced meals to be eaten for a healthier life in the long run. Otherwise, you just add physical problems onto the mental problems which makes it even harder to survive.

Diverticular disease is a condition because of chronic, low fiber diet. Diabetis Mellitus sufferers need good control of their blood sugar to avoid problems. People suffering with Dysphagia have difficulty swallowing and chewing food. This is often a condition from Multiple Sclerosis, Lou Gehrig's Disease, Parkinson's disease, as well as those suffering from dementia. Cardiovascular Disease is the leading cause of death in this country. Lesson it by eating a proper diet. People suffering from this should be on a low fat diet. Often frozen vegetables are off the diet because they have been brined prior to their freeze. Softened water can be very high in salt.Get further information for proper diets and other foods to avoid from your doctor.

If you are helping to feed a person, never feed them when they are lying down. They need to sit up. If they are in a hospital bed, raise it to a sitting position for them. Be watchful to make sure they don't pocket their food in their cheeks. This makes it very difficult to swallow when their mouth is so full of food. Stroke their throats to help encourage them to swallow. General safety procedures, as in a hospital or nursing home, should be followed in the place of residence. Many of the suggestions given are already known, but it is important to review them to have a completely safe kitchen and prepared foods. If people need help with basic issues of life, you can't expect them to know these important factors of living. If they know the facts today, they might not tomorrow.

Practices leading causes to food borne illness are:
1. Failure to properly refrigerate foods.
2. Use a metal stem thermometer.
3. Never thaw by room temperature.
4. Failure to thoroughly heat or reheat food will cause problems.
5. Poor hygiene.
6. Foods prepared a day in advance of service.
7. Raw contaminated foods which are incorporated into foods not cooked.
8. Defrost in bottom shelf of refrigerator in a covered pan.
9. Be careful to avoid cross contamination between foods or food and equipment or hand or food contact on surfaces.

Safe food handling procedures are listed for review also.
1. Watch temperatures.
2. Sanitize food surfaces. Use a tablespoon of bleach to a gallon of water.
3. Use the dishwasher to wash dishes. <u>Never mix bleach with dish detergent or ammonia. This can release toxic fumes that can kill you.</u>
4. Air dry dishes.

CHAPTER THREE

Finding the Right Place
for Them

"We are social beings. The need for others to talk with us, touch us, and respond to us never dies. Even the confused elderly need people contact." This is a remark made by Patricia H. Rushford in her book "The Help, Hope, and Cope Book for People With Aging Parents". We definitely noticed the truth of this when we gave care to the elderly. They most certainly still want to be in life as much as possible, despite their limitations physically or mentally.

This is a newer quandary than in years gone by. In the past, life was different. We have a myth in our psyche that brings a past that was perfect. The legend brings views of quaint homes with white picket fence and all of the family generations living in one home. The doctor comes to the house, by horse or buggy, and tells us grandma has gone on to be with her husband. This is often the pretend world we live in.

In actuality, grandma was probably "gone" long before. If she made it to 60, she no doubt died soon from pneumonia or influenza. In 1900, life expectancy was 47. Only 4% of the people then reached the age of 65. If you lived in the civil war times, you were considered a senior at 40. As we have improved our way of life in improved sanitation, vaccinations, and better nutrition, life expectancy has increased.

The improved length of life has caused great joy, but also concern. Sometimes, families are overwhelmed with the care of loved ones. As families struggle with caretaking responsibilities, there are overwhelming cost concerns too. Nursing homes, along with alternative care, have exploded in recent years because of simple need. Medicaid and Medicare have been brought into our life to help. Hospitals have been penalized if they keep patients in too long. What to do with them? Send them elsewhere for care. With divorce so high, there are fewer full time caregivers available. Our society, without the strengths of church and community, has changed perceptions of family duty.

Help from different living choices need to be made when the elderly need more help.

Questions to ask yourself and family if you are considering moving a loved one:

1. Recognize the danger signs given by elderly people who live independently.
2. Decide together as a family.
3. Plan ahead so decisions will have been made already, helping the process go more smoothly.
4. Don't allow a hospital to make the complete decision for you.
5. Get a full understanding of the person's medical history and diagnosis.
6. Assess medical needs regarding available resources.
7. If a move is decided upon, how do you feel about the placement? Is it clean? Do workers talk with or ignore their patients? Find a place where your loved one is respected and treated as an individual. Visit choices and stay awhile, getting information and observing
8. Realize good alternative places are available.
9. Provide the elderly support as moving decisions are made.
10. Realize this move could be a good decision.

If the move is from a hospital to another living arrangement, here are a few more questions to consider:

1. Is the discharge to be accomplished with medical approval?
2. Has a home-care assessment been undertaken?
3. Is the primary care giver physically and emotionally able to perform the necessary functions?
4. Think twice when the patient has a diagnosis of dementia. Is the place or staff you are considering trained properly for this? Have they taken state training?
5. Are the accommodations suitable for the patient? (If they are in a wheelchair, does the home have ramps, etc.?)
6. Have provisions been made to continue medical treatment as needed?
7. Is this move for the patient's welfare?
8. Is everyone involved in agreement?

When looking for a place for mom or dad, here are six steps to help you:

1. Start with state approved homes.
2. Look at their state inspection reports.
3. Check the housekeeping.
4. Check on the food.
5. Observe patient activities.
6. Observe the staff and their relationship to the residents.
7. If possible, talk to the staff.

You can find these places of help for seniors from a number of sources. Visit the senior center of the town they live in. If your elder is still able, they can visit the center for nutritional lunches, crafts, camaraderie with other seniors, and information regarding their needs from workers. If your city does not have one, visit a neighboring city and their center. They can be a wealth of information to a child seeking to help a parent or loved one. They know of good residences for elders if you have decided that is what is needed. Their knowledge almost always includes assisted living, nursing homes, and adult family homes. Which ones are their favorites?

Why?

Places to call and get information in your area are hospitals, doctors, assisted living homes, adult family homes, rehab centers, nursing homes, and psychiatric hospitals. The following group of terms is from the "Caregivers Handbook" by Visiting Nurses Assoc. of America. You may not need to know these headings, but the knowledge does come in handy if you are trying to seek out a certain need.

"CARE PROFESSIONALS AND WHAT THEY DO:

CARE PROFESSIONAL	LOCATION	SERVICES PROVIDED
Social Worker (Case worker)	Health center/ hospital/home health agency	Assesses the needs of caregiver and the person being cared for. Produces a care plan and guidance on how to obtain services. Coordinates and monitors the care that is provided.
Internist	Health center/ physician's office	A physician who provides general medical advice and treatment, and can refer patients to a specialist, if necessary.
Geriatrician	Health center/ physician's office	A physician with special training in the diagnosis, treatment, and prevention of disorders in older people.
Surgeon	Hospital	A physician who treats disorders by operating. Many surgeons specialize on one part of the body.

CARE PROFESSIONAL	LOCATION	SERVICES PROVIDED
Nurse Practitioner	Health center/ physician's office	Has advanced education and training. Provides general nursing care and may in some regions, diagnose minor complaints and prescribe medicine.
Registered nurse	Health center/ physician's office home health/ agency	Supports the work of the physician, including doing a health assessment, and advising in diet and lifestyle. Carries out clinical procedures, such as wound dressings and injections
Community psychiatric nurse/	Health center or hospital	Provides support and counseling for those with psychiatric problems;
Community mental health nurse	psychiatric unit	Administers medication and monitors overall care and treatment given.
Psychiatric social worker	Social Services or hospital psychiatric unit	Assesses social needs and provides help with practical problems, such as helping a person to fill in an application form for benefits.
Occupational therapist	Social Services	Assesses a person's individual requirements and advice on adapting the home, equipment, and activities to enable him or her to relearn skills and be self-sufficient.

CARE PROFESSIONAL	LOCATION	SERVICES PROVIDED
Physical therapist	Social Services	Treats those with bone and joint problems. Advises on mobility and exercise.
Speech-language pathologist	Health center/ hospital	Treats those with speech and language problems, including stroke victims.
Continence advisor	Health center/ hospital	Provides advice and support, including recommending aids, for those with continence problems.
Stoma care nurse	Health center/ hospital	Provides advice - on skin care and diet, for example - and support for a person who has stoma.
Registered dietitian	Health center/ hospital/ physician's office	Advises on nutrition and healthy diets; tailors special diets to suit specific medical conditions, such as diabetes.
Oncological care	Hospital/ Hospice	Advises on pain and nurse symptom control for cancer patients. Offers care, support, and counseling for patients and caregivers. Organizes short-term care to enable the caregiver to take a break.
Diabetic liaison nurse	Hospital or physician's office	Advises on the effective control of diabetes, as well as overall health matters.

CARE PROFESSIONAL	LOCATION	SERVICES PROVIDED
Podiatrist	Hospital/health center	Offers specialist treatment and therapy for foot problems.
Ambulance personnel	Hospital/Fire department	Provide emergency treatment and transportation to the hospital."

LEVEL OF CARE:

Is home care a realistic alternative? This will affect nearly every aspect of your life. Yet it gives the assurance you might desire. Questions to consider:

1. Will your relative or client need long or short-term care?
2. Will they need constant supervision?
3. Are you the best choice to be their caregiver?
4. How much help can you get from: friends, family, church, social services, or volunteers?
5. What other options do you have if you are not the main caregiver?
6. How will your family be affected?
7. Can you fulfill your current responsibilities in addition to this?
8. Have you made a decision united, as a family?
9. Will you need to do major remodeling in your home?
10. Are you prepared to give up your job, if necessary?

If you are caring for a parent, it can be very distressing as you watch them become frail. We are all reminded of our mortality when they weaken. It might be hard for a parent to accept help from their child, who they have raised and helped along the way. For some, you may feel pressured or guilty that you don't want to take them into your home. Others, may be glad of the possibility to do so. They wouldn't feel right not to do this for their parent. Every person and situation is different.

If you decide to take your loved one into your home, it is a big job, but has benefits for you also. You will often be relied upon to give comfort, support, and reassurance. This will strengthen your relationship, bring you closer. It will also broaden your organizational skills that come in handy for many aspects in other areas of your life. You will be able to take pride and satisfaction that your relative is getting good care. It is not for everyone to do this, so there are other options to consider also.

If you do decide to help on a relative, there is help for you. In addition to the help for taking leave on a job, there are places you can go for help. There are often day centers in the area for seniors. You can take the ill there for a few hours while you go back home to take a nap, go out to lunch, etc.. You need to take care of yourself also. Are you getting enough sleep?

Adult day services   There is socialization provided and caregiver respit. It is all daytime services, including lunch, news, activities, music, occupational therapy such as exercise, drama, and craft work often. Each one is set up differently, so check into what is offered nearby for you. Some also offer hairdressing. Health checks are done at some by visiting nurses. These health checks usually take the temperature, blood pressure, and weight. This can also be a place where you can take your client or relative for the complete day so you can get some much needed rest. Many elders truly enjoy going to these for the opportunity to see friends.

Board and care homes   Housekeeping services and meals are provided in some; aggressive behaviors are not accepted. Minimum supervision is provided.

Assisted living   Housekeeping and meals are provided. Aggressive behaviors are not allowed. This is for people suffering from early stage dementia that need minimal supervision. Surveillance for medicines is given. The rent is often lower priced, so it looks great to take advantage of. But look into it more cautiously. Often times, they have hidden costs, so look into this more carefully. If a worker is needed to help the person to meals, that is an extra cost. Helping people in the bathroom for toileting and showering is another extra cost. Getting your laundry done is also an extra cost. You may be able to get into an assisted living place for $400.00 a month, but consider all of the extra costs that will need to be paid also. Look at the fine print in the documents signed. Is there a length of time a person needs to be there? Are there any attendants at night? This is a must for many elderly, yet in many places, it is also an extra cost.

Homeless shelter   This is for temporary placement until another residence is found that suits the client better. Often early stage dementia is seen. Aggressive behavior is not allowed.

Adult Family Home   This is a residence that takes 1 to 6 clients in their home and helps them in all of their needs. If a client needs help with many issues of life, this may be a place to consider. It depends upon the needs of the client you are trying to find help and another residence for. Usually the adult family home will dress, bathe, feed, entertain, change as needed. In other words, provide all of their daily needs. Some will take clients to the doctor, others not. Some will take severely limited clients, others will not. Get a list of nearby adult family homes from hospitals, doctors, or social services. Then visit these homes and get to know the owners and workers. Find out the types of people in need they will take. Do they take dementia victims only, or also clients that have health, such as stroke, as well as mental challenges? Do you feel comfortable with them? If their home appears clean, ask about the routine and care given to clients. Some adult family homes will only take light dementia clients and others go the full route of helping clients in their home until death. Other questions to ask: What are their capabilities? Are they able to handle the person you are trying to find residence for? Some homes are set up to give enough room for wheelchairs, and others not. Some homes are able to take violent clients, others not. What type of security do they have? Do they provide 24 hour care? Prices may vary upon the needs of the client.

The adult family home gives the client a feeling of family and there are not as many people around. They can have an atmosphere similar to the home they left. This helps suffering people not to get in turmoil so much with the new living arrangement. It seems like moving into another home, not a new huge place to get mixed up in, or get lost in.

Rehab Center Rehabilitation centers are often part of a large medical center. Admission usually comes from recommendations from the hospital. A doctor and specialists in rehabilitation care for patients. Patients are usually stroke victims or from traumatic accidents, some patients needing mechanical ventilation. The patients need to be somewhat strong to work with specialists. Recommendations for placement need to come from doctors.

Nursing Home The federal government recognizes good nursing homes by using the term "skilled nursing facilities". The nursing home is appropriate for people needing chronic and convalescent care. This is sometimes more care than what the adult family home can give, depending upon the specific adult family home. It is a stabilized environment for middle to late stage dementia clients. They have continuous nurse coverage which is sometimes needed. Patients often have a medical condition needing nursing care, along with having dementia. Aggressive behaviors are usually not accepted. Some nursing homes choose not to be Medicare or Medicaid approved, so caution is important when you use those homes. Find out your own information **before placing your loved one.**

The following statement was taken from "Life Worth Living" by William H. Thomas, M. D.

"Current practice in long-term care is based on a confusion of care, treatment, and kindness. Lying at the root of this confusion is the medical model's fixation on diagnosis and treatment. It guarantees that the majority of our resources are spent on the war against disease when, in fact, loneliness, helplessness, and boredom steadily decay our nursing home resident's spirit. A genuine commitment to improving resident's quality of life demands that we correct these problems." When considering nursing homes, think of the experience you have had in visiting them. Reflect on your observations. Think of how you were shown how they take care of people? Was kindness shown? Were their distinct desires considered? Did patients seem to be valued? It depends on where you visited. Some are good, some, not so good. Keep in mind, you are not placing your loved one there to live a long, rich life. They are there because of need. "For nursing home residents, life is therapy, and therapy is life." That quote is taken from "Life Worth Living" by William H. Thomas, M. D. also. Another statement was taken from "Life Worth Living" by William H. Thomas, M. D. "The typical resident of the typical nursing home is bloated with therapy and starving for care." There are good nursing homes out there. You just have to look for them and find one that caters to your specific desires. If you choose a nursing home for your loved one, make sure it is one allowing a lot of close and continued contact with as many people as they desire. Nursing homes that allow animals and plants help encourage people also.

Psychiatric Hospital, Admission is usually restricted to people who are considered a danger to themselves or others. There are short-term inpatient units and longer psychogeriatric units restricted to people whose treatment may be acute because medicines are needed to treat them for episodes they have.

Educate yourself so you can be the best help for your loved one. If a place is chosen, take your loved one, but don't make it a grand outing. Remember, when your are older, change is hard. It may be a fantastic place you have found, but if you make too much out of it, it will frighten and bewilder the patient. They'll get very upset and fight the change. The initial change is very hard, so try and spend as much time with the client there before you leave. Again, talk with workers with the intent of humanizing the person you are leaving.

"If the person with Alzheimer's disease lives alone and receives no regular help, supportive services are strongly encouraged for the sake of safety, companionship, and convenience. Occasional assistance from relatives, neighbors, and friends invariably leaves gaps in the support required. Therefore, hiring someone to assist the person, moving the person into a relative's home, or relocating him or her to an assisted-living facility may be desirable. ... The time line for implementing changes, however, depends on each person's unique situation."

That quote was also found in "Tangled Minds " by Muriel R. Gillick, M. D. Specific care needs to be tailored to meet their specific needs. Find out the model of care that needs to be followed to meet them, and prioritize the care giving goals around them.

What are the common treatment approaches for their needs? If you are looking for someone with dementia, does the place you are considering handle all of the stages of dementia? If not, you will be forewarned you may have to move your loved one another time when the disease progresses.

Is the care facility close to your home, or to other members of the family and/or friends? Demographics play an important part of the consideration, especially if visitors do not desire to travel far, or are unable to travel far themselves. When visiting places to consider, are there any group dynamics, exercise, music, theme days, or other programs that will interest the elderly and keep them as active as possible? Do they serve good, nutritious meals? Do they provide residents a lot of liquids? Nutrition, good hygiene, and possible dehydration are all factors to look for when considering a new residence. Do they keep daily records of the people being cared for? This is especially important if the person being cared for needs to make a surprise trip to the hospital. Doctors will ask, When did they eat last? What did they eat? drink? When was their last bowel movement? Describe. If proper records are not made, these important questions will have no answers.

Observe how the place you are considering takes care of the residents. At the very beginning, as they are discussing plans of care, experience, and you are giving details about the person you will be placing there, they need to make out a care plan. They may not be able to do it completely at entry, but should have it done soon. If they don't, question the place you are considering. This is an important piece of information caregivers need to properly take care of the client. How can they take care of a person if they personally do not know their needs? Some questions you will need to answer so they can take care of the person properly and fully are:

1. What are their mobility abilities
2. Are they able to dress?
3. Are they able to eat alone?
4. Do they need help bathing?
5. Are they continent?
6. Do they have good or poor sight?

7. Can they hear well, or need a hearing aid?
8. What are their behaviors?
9. What are their medications?
10. How do they communicate?
11. How do they manage their finances?
12. What do they like to do socially?
13. What are their hobbies?
14. What is their level of care?
15. What are the objectives of care?

Do they provide activities, music, TV for them if desired? Do they have one on one care given? Interview the caregivers that are not only meeting you, the family, out front, but the caregivers that will actually be taking care of your loved one. Observe their actions. Are you pleased, impressed, or shaken up? If you have questions, now is the time to ask, instead of after you have chosen the place for residence of your loved one. How do they handle violent and aggressive clients? How do they handle wanderers?

Another important point was brought up in "Tangled Minds" by Muriel R. Gillick. "The level of noise, intensity of light, and physical layout are aspects of the physical environment that may affect a resident's behavior. A high noise level often triggers agitated behaviors. The intensity of light in most long-term care facilities is insufficient to ensure the synchronization of circadian rhythms .... It was reported that a higher light intensity promotes the body's secretion of melatonin, which is an important factor in the maintenance of regular sleep patterns ... Caregivers also must modify the environment to ensure care recipients' safety and to support recipients' remaining functional abilities."

The values of people being taken care of is of utmost importance. In considering a residence, what consumer value is given for their choice, dignity, individuality, privacy, and independence? Do the owners and employees have all the training required by the state? If the training certificates are not posted, ask to see them. Is it clean? Are there signs of good housekeeping? This all helps to keep infection down, and should be an important factor to help you decide whether or not you want your loved one there. Then, does the place you are considering meet these needs? Are there any activities for residents? Depending on abilities, seniors usually like some type of structure to their day. Often times, a care area will have a theme for the day. This helps them to look forward to something. Some activities that work well are simple, yet important. Is any reminiscing done? How about music? This often helps to encourage clients, and to have certain memories pertaining to the music they are listening to. Again, I suggest, observe.Try to have them at a place where there is a time of exercise at the place. This will vary from each person depending on their abilities, yet exercise of any kind helps them both physically and mentally.

In making their place of residence safer for them, the hot water tap should be at only 120 degrees. Their sense of feel may be less than yours so they are unable to tell if the water is too hot for them or not. If they are unable to stand for long, a stool should be put in the bathtub for them to sit on. Ask about this. They have a harder time getting up and down safely, so their chairs should be at 18-20 inches from the floor, tables at 30 inches from the floor. Does the place you are considering have the doorways at least 36 inches wide to accommodate wheelchairs if need be. Are there ramps to go to the front door instead of having them use stairs? Make sure the ramp does not exceed 1 inch per foot in length. Going up too steep can cause falls also even though there are no stairs to worry about.

Does the new place you are considering have a plan of action for emergencies? Ask about it. If you are caring for someone who falls, respond, report, and document. Respond by going to them and not having them move. Call 911 and let them be aware of possible need. Don't let them drink anything. Do for the injured one as directed by 911. Report to another family member, caseworker, and/or supervisor of the area if you are away from home. Hopefully, no big injuries have occurred, but 911 attendants can give you more professional advice regarding that than you would have without them. Document this fall. This helps others caring for the person to know what to be careful about so other falls can be avoided.

Retirement communities, for the most part, are started for independent, healthy older people. Some have added a nursing area, but most do not have extra help. Services, such as bathing, are extra cost. Continuing care retirement centers are for older people that are reasonably healthy, but realize they will need more help as time goes by. Assisted living facilities are usually apartment-style living homes to serve those needing daily help with just a little bit of medical needs. Many states do not require them to be licensed. They usually give twenty-four hour security, two or three meals a day, housekeeping, laundry, emergency call buttons, transportation, activities, and assistance with medication, bathing, dressing, and toileting. The more help needed, the more expensive the cost. Nursing homes and adult family homes are geared for people needing total supervision, twenty-four hours a day, seven days a week. Contact the Alzheimer's Association, and other health agencies for information and booklets to help guide you in placing the loved one in the correct housing.

Daniel Kuhn, M. S. W. wrote in "Alzheimers Early Stages" the following paragraphs. "If a confused person refuses to give up her independence and move into a safer setting, understanding something of what she may be thinking and feeling may help make the move easier. A move from independent living to living with someone else may mean giving up one's independence and admitting one's impairment. Moving means more losses. It means giving up a familiar place and often many familiar possessions. That place must show the realization that possessions are the tangible symbols of one's past and reminders when one's memories fail."

"In the late phase of the disease, (Alzheimer's) patients are totally dependent on others for their care, including eating and hygiene. People caring for them need to use simple words and sentences, and need to be observant of the patient's responses in order to figure out what they want and how they feel.

'At some point, family members must decide whether the person with Alzheimer's disease can be taken care of properly at home. In some situations this is possible, but requires obtaining reliable outside help. The alternative is nursing home placement. In our experience, family members often resist this, because they feel the patient will be unhappy and poorly cared for. In fact, if a nursing home is a good one (and there are many) the patient will receive good care and may benefit greatly from the company of others and daily programs that are geared to his or her level of ability. In addition, the family member is freed to spend quality time with the patient, rather than getting exhausted by the quantity of time required for hour-to-hour care.'...

'Alzheimer's disease can be a frighteningly complicated problem to handle. To reduce the burden as much as possible, take advantage of any and all available help. The first step is to be well informed. The Alzheimer's Association, the primary advocacy group within the United States, acts as a clearing-house for comprehensive and reliable information." Other options are assisted living (with little help) and adult family homes (with varied help). Visit the closest hospital and speak with social workers, discharge planners, and health directors for activities and health suggestions. If you can get someone to help you in addition to their busy schedule, it will be a great help. Ask the physical therapist for specific exercises for the client you care for. Ask the social worker for suggestions regarding the sick one's abilities for the activities you have planned. Verify that it will be all right, not too strenuous. Does the place you were considering moving your loved one to show an active sense about the importance for daily, although limited, physical exercise? Verify the care you desire. Will they do all of it? How do you feel about the caregivers?, their workers? For the move to be a success, you have to feel comfortable with the place you have chosen. It is too easy for your loved one you are caring for to pick up on concerns you have.

Visit or call their doctor with your questions and concerns. They will often have a list of numbers for you to call if they can't give you complete information. Find out from their doctor what is needed. Can they go into an assisted living home if the family is unable to help? Do they need more help, like an adult family home can provide, or are they at the near end where they need medical help found only in hospitals or nursing homes? Pin the doctor down to get an informed answer. Change is so hard for the elderly, it is best if you can take them to the correct facility for their needs instead of moving them around immediately after placing them somewhere else.

Contact the state health department and they can give you

further information on places to take your loved one. They can send you a list of Assisted Living, Adult Family Homes, and Nursing Homes in your area for you to consider. Ask their opinions and get feedback they have regarding any you are interested in. Often, they will have some information regarding the specific place you are interested in.

Visit Adult Family Homes in the area to see if they would fit in with your loved one's needs. They are smaller and can often have a home-like atmosphere that is more comforting to some, especially those against change. It depends upon the adult family home as to what type of clients they will take. For participants there, they can provide one on one care that is very desirous for many people. When visiting, notice how the workers and owners interact with clients. Is it clean? Do they serve healthy meals with snacks? Are there any activities for the elderly planned? Are their training certificates posted clearly for you to see? Ask them about their training specialties. Do they fit into what you are looking for? These are just a few questions you can ask at the visit that will give you more information to help you make the right decision. If you have a question pop into your mind when visiting, ask. If you think of it driving home, call them and verify the information you need. Call previous families that have used the facility to get their feelings and opinions on the home. All of these questions seem endless now, but will help you in the long run to make the right choice.

Wherever you place them, it is important to keep in touch with them. They will most certainly wonder what has happened, or why they have been placed where they are, but your visits will calm them down, and encourage them this is the right place for them to be. If you wonder about something, ask the care givers privately about the concern. They are with the patient twenty four hours a day, seven days a week, and are more aware of changes in your loved one. Questions to ask:

1. What foods will they be fed? Will they receive help to eat, if needed?
2. What activities will they be shown?
3. Will they be given help, if needed, in all aspects of life?

(dressing, bathing, toileting, eating, entertainment)

When you meet the specific caregivers, and see the home, there will be other questions that pop into your mind. Ask away. Don't be frightened away by the enormous task before you. What can you do to be more prepared?

What should you do to get more insight regarding the future? What should you do when you get too tired?

CHAPTER FOUR

Getting Burned Out

*"In any helping relationship, the personality values,
attitudes, and beliefs of the helper are of primary importance."*
Gary R. Collins, *"How To Be A People Helper"*

Whether you are taking care of your loved one, are hired to care for another person, have an adult family home or nursing home or assisted care home that you work at part time or full time or own and run twenty four hours, seven days a week, you will need help. If you don't, you will get burned out. You may love working in the field, love helping people, love one on one work, but if you don't have help, you will become over burdened and have to stop completely, because it is too overwhelming of a job to do constantly, even if you have a few dependable people that are like yourself and constantly working also. They need breaks too. Burn out sounds rather debasing to a hard worker and owner, but that is what happens. Just as other people have eight hour or plus jobs, you can't expect to be in top form for yourself, the clients, and everyone else if you don't get the proper rest yourself. You begin to hate the job, or at least aspects about it. You no longer find happiness in the job of helping people like at first.

On any given day, we don't know who will walk into our lives, or what problem we may come up against. These problems can be regarding yourself, your family, your friends, or your workmates.

Life moves more easily when we can remember to realize these three points. Put them into operation in your life regarding clients, families, and workers.

These important questions to ask were brought up in "Healing Conversations - What To Say When You Don't Know What To Say" by Nanci Guilmartin. "What keeps you from pausing long enough to wonder what might be going on in another person's world?

How could you get curious about what might be on the other person's plate that is making that person's life (and maybe yours) difficult?

What would you have to do for yourself to switch to a slower gear so that you can hear what others are saying, what they're not saying, and what they wish it was safe to say to you about whatever is troubling them at that moment?"

When working with sick people, you need to be open and helpful as patients, family members, and medical personnel speak with you. Is your job part time, full time, or live in?

Your job will bring sadness to family members, and to yourself,. especially when the client they love and you have cared for passes away. It is important for you, as a worker, to guard against depression, so you can do your job to the best of your ability; being an encourager for clients in their last days and visiting family alike.

People who are depressed don't see the world as it really is. They develop errors in thinking and unrealistic attitudes about themselves and life. As a worker for the elderly, try to have your goal be to help families and clients see and feel the reality of life and how they can cope with it's changes. This takes time. Listen to their talk as they share their sadness, feelings, and thoughts about the whole process of loss. Sometimes it will seem as if you have gone one step forward and two steps back. You must not ignore negative or positive experiences, but build upon them because conflict can be good. It can help you measure where you are at and help you go forward.

Depression is a feeling within us that we always have, just as we have other feelings also, of happiness, sadness, joy, anger, etc.. It is up to you in how you handle it. We may go in and out of depressions like we go in and out of the house. It is like the common cold or flu that hits you at any time. What we do with these feelings and problems can be short or take a long period of time. It depends on how we live with it. We can live with depression or die from it. No matter what you do, depression is a part of life. As long as we live in this world, we are going to deal with and face depression.

The only way out of depression is to know Jesus Christ, because He is our ticket out of the world. Knowing Jesus Christ as your personal savior and Lord is the only way for you to overcome depression. He gives us hope. When we accept Him as our savior, it gives us hope for the future with the knowledge that our sins; past, present, and future, are forgiven, and the fact that He gives us such great anticipation for the future. If you believe in God, it doesn't mean you'll have clear sailing. Because we have to live in this world, we will face depression until the Lord takes us out of this world.

Here is an acrostic on depression to help you deal with it:

Decision: The person has to make a decision they are depressed and they have a problem and want help. They have to make a decision for Jesus Christ and let the Holy Spirit command them. If people make this decision and follow through with it, they will change their life and their outlook on life's experiences.

Exercise: You need to get in shape. A strong body helps your mind to think on healthy things and do good thinking. It is well known that a healthy body is less susceptible to mental as well as physical illness.

Prayer: To overcome depression, you must be in prayer and have other people praying for you.

Routine: It will help your life go more smoothly when you set a routine for your life; one that involves God. Build a strong structure in your life that includes Him and Christian fellowship.

Encouragement: Seek to be with people who will encourage you and build you up. Get a support group that you can be accountable to. This time of change can be a positive and maturing path in your life if you allow it to be so.

Self worth: You must build up your self worth. You know that is going to take time most likely, and you are not alone. When you are positive regarding yourself, you can be positive with other people and motivate them forward.

<u>S</u>piritual We need help and guidance; with health information - regarding our body and the body of others, and with spiritual matters - regarding our relationship toward God and other's relationship to Him.. Depression is also a spiritual battle. We need to be in His word and in prayer to receive the guidance to go on.

<u>I</u>mage: We must know we are created in the image of God and we are a child of the King. When you are going through tough times with your family member who is sick, or at work with the elderly, realize you are human and are going to fail sometimes and be down. Yet if we remember our foundation, we can have hope and faith in the Lord to help us back up despite the enormous losses we are feeling.

<u>O</u>pen: We must be open minded to God's path in our life at this time. We should challenge our way of thinking and learn new coping techniques to handle depression.

<u>N</u>eeds: We must pull our mind away from ourselves and on to the needs of others. We need to focus our thoughts on God for encouragement and guidance and in helping others in need.

Since we get information so quickly and things are happening in this world so fast, we also go into depression fast, and then on to the next depression before we get over the first. The feelings and emotions may keep building up and going down, if we don't guard against it. Our recovery period gets longer if our depression keeps building.

We must help people with depression in their way of thinking about themselves and life. Also, their attitudes about life and what is happening around them should be discussed. If depressed, go to a counselor. There, they (and you) can get excited about possible change. They can get encouraged further if you help them set attainable goals for themselves.

If you work at a nursing home, assisted care, or adult family home on a part time basis, it will be easier for you to leave. You will wonder about the people when you are at home or with family and friends. You can even think of better ways to do your job during your leisure time. For the family involved, support groups for

Alzheimer patients are beginning to take hold. There are also work groups and recreational groups available in some cities, colleges, churches. Use community resources. Encourage families to visit, with their children.

Training in dementia should be given to everyone helping to take care of the older person. Otherwise, there is too much strain taken upon owners, workers, staff of any type. If workers are not on the same road map on how to properly take care of these clients, there will be many disruptions and misunderstandings. That is already going on in the client's life. They don't need to witness it constantly with staff also. Daniel Kuhn, from "Alzheimer's Early Stages" brought out this important truth. "Training in managing behaviors in dementia should not be limited to nursing staff. All employees - including housekeeping and dietary staff, rehabilitation therapists, activity therapists, social workers, and office staff (Kaplan, 1966a) - who interact with people with dementia need a basic knowledge of dementing illnesses, an understanding of the philosophy of the dementia program, and the ability to use appropriate communication skills and behavior management techniques."

Do you ever have days that go downhill right from the start? Are there weeks and months you feel this way also? Sometimes it is from living with the realities of life such as in chronic pain, or working with people who suffer from this. If you are having these troubles, you need to accept them, not live around them. Sometimes we make it our goal in life to live pain free. It is great if we can accomplish that, but it is often not possible, for yourself, your client, or loved one you're trying to help. When there is constant pain, even in slight amounts, your life is thrown off balance. You often cannot remember people's names, or other important aspects of the day. We need to learn to accept that pain, physical and/or emotional, is sometimes a part of our life, whether we are feeling it ourselves, or know of someone else suffering. Should we feel like we're failures if getting rid of the pain isn't possible? It is not right for us to feel this way because life is not perfect. If we are not in pain regarding something, someone else is. When our space in life together is over, what should victory look like? This is different for everyone.

When you are comforting someone with a chronic condition, here are some guidelines to help from "Healing Conversations - What To Say When You Don't Know What To Say" by Nance Guilmartin. " Please don't make asking us about our health your first question. We are more than our condition. If we need to tell you how we're feeling, we'll let you know. If you've discovered new information about our condition, please don't be offended if we don't follow up right away or even take your suggestions. After trying many approaches, we may (temporarily) have run out of energy to try something else; we're tired of getting our hopes up. Days or months later, however, your information may be just what we need. Even if there are activities that we can no longer do with you, maybe there's a way we can still enjoy being with you: If we can't ski, we can read by the fire; if we can't paddle, we can ride along in a double kayak; if we can't dance, we can still enjoy music! Please realize that although our condition may not improve, it helps if we can make as much out of our life as we can instead of focusing on what we can't do."

Further good information in responding with other employees and the clients you work with was found later in "Healing Conversations - What To Say When You Don't Know What To Say" by Nance Guilmartin. "It's more important to understand the situation than to be right. Take the time to step into someone else's shoes if you want to understand what went wrong. Even if you are right, would you rather be right or in relationship with your customer (client)? Pause to get your breath when someone is yelling at you, because at first all you want to do is yell back, interrupt to explain, or fix the problem fast. A few deep breaths give you "breathing room" for perspective.

When someone's venting at you, all you can do is listen. The person isn't ready to hear what you have to say until he feels he's been heard and understood. You don't have to admit that your company or you is to blame, but you can say you are sorry it is happening. Do what you can to make things right for the customer (or client) while honoring the customer's dignity and your company's budget and principles. Once you know what went wrong, explain the cause of the problem graciously, giving the customer (client) a chance to save face while acknowledging that we're all human and mistakes happen." These hints are for working outside of the home most likely, but they can also be helpful to you as you work with your client, and others involved with that person.

What can you do specifically to make a client happier?

CHAPTER FIVE

Being a People Helper

"The best people helpers are those who practice their helping
skills and who are involved in the lives of others."
from "How To Be A People Helper" Gary R. Collins

I couldn't resist putting the following poem "A Woman" by Maya Angelou. It was shared by a friend when I was having a stressful time. She was a great people helper for me, and probably didn't even realize it. Hopefully, it will bring back the laughter and encouragement for you also.

A Woman, by Maya Angelou

When I was in my younger days,
I weighed a few pounds less,
I needn't hold my tummy in
to wear a belted dress.

But now that I am older,
I've set my body free;
There's comfort of elastic
Where once my waist would be.

Inventor of those high heeled shoes

My feet have not forgotten;
I have to wear a nine now,
But used to wear a seven.

And how about those pantyhose -
They're sized by weight, you see,
So how come when I put them on
The crotch is at my knee?

I need to wear these glasses
As the print's been getting smaller;
And it wasn't very long ago
I know that I was taller.

Though my hair has turned to gray
and my skin no longer fits,
On the inside, I'm the same old me,
It's the outside's changed a bit.

But, on a positive note ...

I've learned that no matter what happens or how bad it seems
today, life does go on, and it will be better tomorrow.

I've learned that you can tell a lot about a person by the
way he/she handles these three things: a rainy day, lost
luggage, and tangled Christmas tree lights.

I've learned that regardless of your relationship
with your parents, you'll miss them when they're gone
from your life.

I've learned that making a "living" is not the same thing as
making a "life".

I've learned that life sometimes gives you a second chance.
I've learned that you shouldn't go through life with a

catcher's mitt on both hands. You need to be able to throw something back.

I've learned that whenever I decide something with an open heart,
I usually make the right decision.
I've learned that every day you should reach out and touch someone.
People love a warm hug, or just a friendly pat
on the back.

I've learned that I still have a lot to learn.
I've learned that people will forget what you said,
people will forget what you did,
but people will never forget
how you made them feel.

Please send this on to five phenomenal women today.
If you do, something good will happen ....
You will boost another woman's self esteem.

If you don't .... the elastic will break and your panty hose will fall down around your knees.

1. **Why by a people helper?**

A simple reason for this would be because you love that person. They are part of your family. They are your neighbor. They are your best friend's parents. They are an acquaintance from work. You enjoy encouraging people, any people, that come along your life's road. You have chosen a life's work that uses encouragement as an active part of the job. There are so many reasons to help others. Some are: encouragement, the way you were brought up, gratification for self as you help others, you love to motivate, cheer up, hearten others that are down. Whatever the reason, people thrive on encouragement, on positive input. Unless otherwise indicated, Bible quotations are taken from the New International Version of the bible, published by Zondervan Publishing House, copyright

1990. "An anxious heart weighs a man down, but a kind word cheers him up." That is found in Proverbs 12:25. In some ways, many of us spend more time in looking for the "big things" to help people. We forget about the little things we can do. This might simply be a smile, nod of the head, a nice comment "you look nice today", "that color looks good on you", "your perfume smells nice on you", "you were a great help, thanks" etc. It's easy to take these comments for granted, but surprising how much they lift the listener's spirits.

A people helper can be someone who is non professional or in a trained position. They can be at any age but the older the helper is, the more effective they seem to be, because they have experience in dealing with life and the problems that come to all. Sometimes we try so hard to do something big for someone, we miss out on what life is all about; storing up treasures in heaven that will last for eternity. Everyone can have an influence on a person who is close to them. They can focus on one person at a time.

There are a lot of people helpers in the bible great and small. One of the small people helpers is small only because of it's length and mention in the bible. It still made a big impact on someone's life. It was Commander Naaman's young servant maiden. Her name was not mentioned in II King's 5, but she helped by informing her master that prophet Elisha could heal him of leprosy. It was the faith of that young servant of God that shared her faith and belief to Naaman that made him go to Elijah where he was healed of his leprosy. It was because of her faith in God that Naaman became a believer. As the song goes, "It only take a spark to get a fire going." We all can help make a difference in people's lives.

Some of the qualities needed to be an effective people helper are: **H**umility, **E**ncouragement, **L**ove, **P**atience, **E**mpathy, and **R**espect.

Humility is to see people as God sees them and you. Unless otherwise indicated, Bible quotations in this paragraph are taken from the New International Version, © 1990, by Zondervan Publishing House. This is taught to us in the bible especially at Roman's 12:16 and Philippians 2:3 through 5. Romans 12:16 "Live in harmony with one another. Do not be proud, but be willing to associate with people of low position." Philippians 2:-5. "Your attitude should be the same as that of Christ Jesus." Let the word of God and His wisdom come out of your humility. People will then see your true colors and know that you care. This is so encouraging for someone in need. The **Encouragement** and **Empathy** you give should be from your heart.

Then it is helpful and meaningful. The Lord commanded us to encourage one another. This truth is found in Hebrews 10:24, 25. Unless otherwise indicated, Bible quotations are from the New International Version © 1990. "And let us consider how we may spur one another toward love and good deeds. Let us not give up meeting together, as some are in the habit of doing, but let us encourage one another and all the more as you see the Day approaching."

Love is another quality people helpers must have. We are commanded to love one another as the Lord has loved us. That love covers a multitude of sins and we must show and have agape' love that endures forever and never fails. We should be **p**atient in helping others. Patience is listening to the whole story and understanding what they are saying. Sometimes, with the elderly, because of changing lifestyles and health problems, this is hard to do. You can't jump to your own conclusion, but be patient and listen until you understand the big picture of what they are trying to communicate. Only then can we tend to them correctly. These truths are found in James 1:19, I Thessalonians 5:14-15. Unless otherwise indicated, Bible quotations are taken from the New International Version, Zondervan Publishing House, © 1990. James 1:19 "My dear brothers, take note of this: Everyone should be quick to listen, slow to become angry, for man's anger does not bring about the righteous life that God desires." I Thessalonians 5:14-15 "And we urge you brothers, warn those who are idle, encourage the timid, help the weak, be patient with everyone. Make sure nobody pays back wrong for wrong, but always try to be kind to each other and to everyone else." New ideas for the world we live in?

We must also show **E**mpathy to the people we are helping. Then the person will see you are truly concerned for them and sense you are doing your best. The person you are helping will finally understand you have good intentions and are trying to see the problem from their point of view. Having this mutual sensitivity helps you both build a good rapport with one another and you can be an effective helper even more.

You need to also use **R**espect when helping people. The person you help respects you by trusting you to help them. You must respect the person's rights and keep their information confidential from other clients. This lesson on trust is learned from verses I Peter 2:17, I Timothy 3:8. Unless otherwise indicated, Bible quotations are taken from the New International Version, Zondervan Publishing House, © 1990. I Peter 2:17: "Show proper respect to everyone. Love the brotherhood of believers, fear God, honor the king." I Timothy 3:8 "Deacons, likewise, should be men of respect, sincere, not indulging in wine, and not pursuing dishonest gain."

Being a people helper in a crisis is very challenging, yet rewarding. In scripture, we can see how Jesus, the greatest people helper, handled the crisis situation with Lazarus. Jesus first listened to the sister, and got an idea of how He would handle the situation. Secondly, He gave the sisters of Lazarus hope and comfort. They put their faith in Jesus because they knew He could do something. This is the same when we are helping someone. We can give hope and guidance through prayer, listening, and actions.

When helping people in crisis, we must be in control of ourselves. We must be equally balanced emotionally, spiritually, and physically. If we are not, we present little help. We must show the person that we are calm and knowledgeable in what is going on, and in what is needed. In some situations, the crisis will never be resolved completely, even by taking action. When someone discovers the existence of an incurable disease, or looses a loved one in death, the crisis may bring permanent change. As people helpers, we are there to help people, not to show them how good we are or to tell them how they should feel. We need to listen to them and point them to help. We should help them find fellowship at this hard time, and pray for them.

Some points from "God's Words Of Life", written by Sharon Mahoe, are very enlightening. "So many times in the past few weeks I had come home to hear a message of encouragement on my answering machine: 'Thinking of you;' 'I love you.' Day after day, when hysteria and raw emotions were my constant companions I found the incredible support and concern of friends every time I needed someone.

'Encouragement has never filled a flat tire. Encouragement has never made a car payment, nor fixed a broken washing machine. But encouragement from another gives us the strength to do what we feel we cannot do, hold on when we feel we cannot hold on, and try what we might not dare to try.

'Encouragement. Doesn't sound like much, but it's everything. Send some encouragement today. You'll be part of someone's memories for a long, long time."

Remember the person you are concerned about. Their life is changing in a dramatic way. They remember the past, and run to catch up with it. It's gone, and many of their abilities with it

"I am hungry for the life that is being taken away from me .... I hunger for friendship, happiness, and the touch of a loved hand. What I ask for is that what is left of my life shall have some meaning." James Thomas wrote that in "The Loss of Self.", published by ABC-CLIO.

2. **The joy of being a people helper:**

Why choose to be a teacher, doctor, nurse, pastor? These are just a few helping jobs that come to mind. There are hundreds more. Why choose to work at restaurant, store, be a counselor? It is because we all are different, and are driven to follow our dreams. Yet each of these jobs can bring joy to others. Consider the job you have now. It may not bring out in your mind a job that necessarily helps people, or brings out joy, but it could easily fit the bill because everyone is different and needs different assistance.

3. **How to be a people helper:**

In caring for people, make sure the place you work in is prepared for emergencies. If you are running a personal home to take care of the elderly, whether it is for one person or six, you need to be prepared for the unexpected. Find out what emergencies are most likely to happen in your area. Figure out a way to be prepare for each of these possibilities. Meet with workers and families of clients and discuss what you will do to prepare for an emergency and what your actual actions would be if that emergency does happen. Practice what you have discussed. Monthly practice emergency exits are advisable so everyone knows what to do if needed, and is comfortable (used to) the actions.

Know the best way to contact families if an emergency does happen. Pick out two meeting places to go to if the home needs to be evacuated. Post emergency phone numbers by the phone. Know yourself and then show workers how to and when to shut off water, gas, and electricity at main switches. Install smoke detectors and test them monthly to make sure they are working properly.

Learn first aid and CPR. Contact your fire department to learn of home fire hazards you may not have thought of. Meet with neighbors so everyone is in agreement as to what would be done next if an emergency did happen.

Make sure your home or place of residence for the loved one has enough emergency water and food, along with a first aid kit. When making a list of items to take out in an emergency, remember the ones with special needs and have a way to practice grabbing these items up quickly.

Some for elderly would be: heart and blood pressure medication, insulin, prescription drugs, denture needs, contact lenses and supplies, and extra eye glasses. If there is time, grab up games and books to keep them busy and amused until everything is back to normal. Keep these emergency supplies on hand also: flashlights and batteries, bottled water and juice, canned food, non-electric can opener, matches and candles, blankets, a portable radio with extra batteries.

Know all the evacuation routes.

When emergency concerns are taken care of, here are also some suggestions for general caregiving and being a people helper:

1. Be informed about the patient's illness. How does it affect them? How does it affect your views on them? How does it affect their safety? Are they able to take their own medicine safely? Get an assessment on them done by a doctor or

nurse trained in this. The resident assessment includes their heritage, childhood, personality information, favorite items in their life, recreational treats, places traveled, pets, favorite foods, holidays celebrated, significant achievements, significant traumas/tragedies, things loved and hated. With this information, the caregiver can be attuned to what caregiving tasks will work best.

2. Share your concerns with the patient. Are they able to fix their own meals safely? Are they getting the right food, in regard to their illness? Often senior centers fix well balanced meals that will even be changed for diabetics and other people with different food needs if this is shared with them. Would the patient be able to safely go out for an outing there? If so, this provides them with a well balanced meal and good companionship with other elders, and visiting people of all ages.

3. Try to solve your most frustrating problems one at a time.

4. Get enough rest yourself.

5. Use your common sense and imagination.

6. Maintain a sense of humor.

7. Try to establish an environment that allows as much freedom as possible but also offers the structure that confused people need. Are there any supplies or equipment needed they specifically need? Any props?

8. Remember to talk to the confused person.

9. Have an ID necklace or bracelet made for the confused person.

10. Keep the impaired person active but not upset. From the assessment, caregivers can find out the response capabilities and structure their activities around that. Too much activity will sometimes mean too much stimulation and too much confusion. Answering the previous questions will help sustain the patient safely. Usually always, visiting family helps to encourage the confined person. Having sons, daughters, and grandchildren visit helps the elderly to know they are not completely forgotten, even if they live in a different place now. Some families have a hard time visiting

the elderly, but encourage them to do so because of the emotional benefits the visits have.

Besides having trouble with speech and communication, the individual may also suffer from loss of coordination, and loss of sense of time. With Alzheimer's disease, they have definite problems with many functions of life. One of these is speech. Oftentimes, how we hear someone determines, to a certain extent, our understanding of them. When Alzheimer's disease gets worse, most patient have repetitive speech. This can really wear the caregiver down. These obsessive requests means extra duty for you, the caregiver. Why they repeat so often is deep down they fear they will forget their own request. Every moment their minds challenge them to remember, and each moment they are forgetting something else. Alzheimer patients may ask the same two, three, or four questions daily. We, as listeners, get tired of this. We can only approach this problem with sensitivity. The patients are reassured by our consistent answers to their repetitive questions. A very observant acknowledgment was brought out by Guy McKhann, M. D. and Marilyn Albert Ph. D. in "Keeping Your Brain Young". "Whether they know it or not, patients are conducting surveys, trying to figure out what has changed and what has stayed the same."

Patients with Alzheimer's in the early stages definitely have trouble with communication. You can see and hear it a number of ways. They may have difficulty finding the right words, comprehending abstract language, or talking on the phone. They will often repeat questions or statements that seem to get 'stuck' in their minds. They will also often digress, have difficulty solving problems, and get very mixed up when there are too many sights and sounds that seem to be coming at them from all angles.

When speaking to them, treat them as a real person. Communicate slowly and calmly. Be positive and reassuring. Allow them to complete statements instead of interrupting. Avoid words with special meanings for them. Learn the meaning of certain words the patient uses all of the time. Speak clearly and slowly maintain contact. If you are trying to educate them regarding anything, tell them what to expect. Match your actions with your words. Talk about and name emotions being felt, "I see you are upset".

Repeat to them enjoyable activities they have done. Mention male and female tasks they may have done in the past to help them relive it. Some chores may still be done by them and they enjoy doing them, if it is physically possible for them to do it. No one likes to think they are useless. For men, did they use to polish their shoes and boots? They still may be able to do this, depending on their abilities. Can they still play cards? Did they used to do any woodworking? Could they still do this? For women, there are all of the familiar kitchen tasks. Can they still cut coupons? Can they dry utensils? Can they do any sewing safely? Can they work with flowers? Can they still fold clothes and towels? Don't argue with them because they may not understand your reasoning and arguments really don't solve anything at this point in their life. Instead, maintain a soothing environment and redirect activity. They may be at the point where they need repetition. If so, come back and begin again.

Another important point when working with this group of people was brought out again in the book "Keeping Your Brain Young" by Guy McKhann, M. D. and Marilyn Albert Ph. D. "Slang adds to the existing confusion and stress that many caregivers feel. Remember, caregivers are already dealing with subject changes, stories, questions, parroting, repetition, speech apraxia, dysarthria, and more."

One caregiver admitted, "It's only eight o'clock in the morning, and I'm exhausted."

Sentimentality disappears when Alzheimer's strikes. The patient may use hurtful speech unlike the loving speech they used to use. Others use aggressive speech, different from the past, and the use of refrains.

Body language and gestures are important to use when working with your client. It is almost like a second language for them. Caregivers must know their patients and be inventive. Alzheimer's Association coordinator Bobbie Speich, L. P. N., N. H. A., discussed body language at the Mayo Clinic's first annual conference on Alzheimer's disease, and her points are summarized here:

1. Use an open stance and gestures. Don't approach a patient

with your hands in your pockets.
2. Be cautious about putting your arm around a patient. The patient may think you are trying to restrain him or her and start to struggle.
3. Never approach a patient from the rear, which may be interpreted as a threat. However, approaching the patient from an angle may work.
4. Mimic the actions you want the patient to take, such as the various steps in brushing and rinsing teeth.
5. Make eye contact and look concerned. You want to transmit the message, "I care about you."
6. Nod your head while the patient is talking to show you are listening.

Whether the patient is ill or not, many aging people become angry at the reality of growing older. They may have anger at living with their child, at being old, or at unresolved issues. You never fully know what is on someone else's plate. It is easier and smoother in the long run to accept their anger quietly instead of returning language the same way they are yelling at you.

You may be angry inside, but cool off long enough to know they are coming from another level of life than you are.

You can also help your communication with loved ones with dementia by:

1. Gaining their attention,
2. Cutting down on background noise
3. Using your nonverbal cues with them
4. Maintain a calm tone and atmosphere
5. Listen sincerely to them and encourage them with your expression
6. Encourage comprehension. Did they understand you? If not, reword conversation.
7. Distract them as needed to get them back on conversation needed at that time.
8. Help them by giving gentle reminders
9. Help them out with their problems. How can you help solve

them?

10. If they don't want to talk, sit companionably and quietly with them.

You can't control the swiftness or slowness of their illness. It's their problem. Don't let your anger at their inabilities foreshadow the need for help they do have. Be compassionate, bite your lip, and help.

Regarding food for them, nutrition is very important. Just as with a growing child, food plays an important role in keeping older people healthier too. From the grain group they should have 6 to 11 servings, from the vegetable group 3 to 5 servings, from the fruit group, 2 to 4 servings, from the milk group, 2 to 3 servings, and from the meat group 2 to 3 servings.

Everyone is an individual, and you can't force the food down them. At certain points of illness, it will be almost impossible for them to eat or for you to feed them. Yet it is important to try to keep the variety of foods in them. If they don't like chicken, give them ham instead, or another meat substance. Try different ways of fixing vegetables so they will eat them. This will be healthier for them, and for you too if you are sharing the meal.. If they don't like milk, it's possible they like ice cream. Mixing and matching the foods for a healthy diet will give them variety with their meals and meet the health guidelines for them at this time in their life. For different diseases, different menus are needed. This is especially true for Diabetis, Parkinson's disease, and for heart disease patients. Pause to consider the one you are caring for and are concerned about. They probably would do better with a good diet also. This is a must for depressed people and people with dementia. Drugs can cause nutritional deficiencies so it is important to find out from your doctor or pharmacist how the medicine will affect a person so it can be counteracted with other foods. If weight continues to be lost, a person should seek out a dietitian for an assessment and create a nutritional meal plan. Also, it is important to provide well balanced meals for a healthier life in the long run. Otherwise, you just add physical problems onto the mental problems which makes it even harder to survive.

Diverticular disease is a condition because of chronic, low fiber diet. Diabetis Mellitis sufferers need good control of their blood sugar to avoid problems. People suffering from Dysphagia have difficulty swallowing and chewing food. This is often a condition from Multiple Sclerosis, Lou Gehrig's disease, Parkinson's disease, as well as those suffering from dementia. Cardiovascular Disease is the leading cause of death in this country. Lesson it by eating properly. People suffering from this should be on a low fat diet. Often frozen vegetables are off the diet because they have been brined prior to the freeze. Softened water can be very high in salt. Get further information for proper diets and other foods to avoid from your doctor.

If you are helping to feed a person, never feed them when they are lying down. They need to sit up for proper digestion. If they are in a hospital bed, raise it to a sitting position. Be watchful to make sure they don't pocket their food in their cheeks. This makes it difficult to swallow when their mouth is so full of food. Stroke their throats to help encourage them to swallow.

General safety procedures, as in a hospital or nursing home, should be followed in the place of residence. Many of the suggestions given are already known, but it is important to review them to have a completely safe kitchen and prepared foods. If people need help with basic issues of life, you can't expect them to know these important factors of living. If they know the facts today, there is no promise they'll know them tomorrow.

The following is a food chart I used when running my adult family home. When I showed it to their doctors, they were pleased with it and encouraged me to continue it's use. Important vitamins to concentrate on are calcium, magnesium, potassium, phosphorus, iron, zinc, vitamin A, vitamin B, Vitamins B6 and B12, vitamin C, vitamin D, vitamin E, and vitamin K. Each of these specific foods also help the aging person: fish, oats, bananas, fiber, cranberry juice and purple grape juice.

FOOD CHART

These foods and liquids fight **<u>CANCER</u>**: watermelon, tomatoes, raspberries, red bell peppers, pumpkin, apples, apricots, nectarines, tomatoes, beets, blueberries, bran cereal, olive oil, broccoli, brown rice, brussel sprouts, prunes, cabbage, vitamin C, carrots, cauliflower, vitamin E, vitamin A, coffee, purple grape juice, milk, tea, wine.

Besides helping fight cancer, apples help keep bones strong.

CALCIUM helps build bones. You learn from the Fundamentals of Caregiving handbook that "Calcium plays a role in bone and tooth formation, blood clotting, heart rhythm, nerve transmission, muscle growth and contraction, proper functioning of cell membranes." Calcium also helps sustain intestinal contractions and sustain heart rhythm needed for growth and proper movement of muscles. Calcium also helps blood to clot and works to keep teeth and bones healthy. It is found in apples, onions, wheat, corn, rice, apricots, berries, cherries, grapes, oranges, pears, broccoli, carrots, tomatoes, beans, 2% milk, cheese, yogurt, ice cream, watermelon, fish, raisins, strawberries, nuts, green, leafy vegetables, figs, and yogurt.

MAGNESIUM fights heart disease, lowers blood pressure, fights depression. Informative information on magnesium is found in the "2001 Current Medical Diagnosis & Treatment Book" by Lawrence M. Tierney, Jr., Stephen J. McPhee, and Maxine A. Papadakis . "It is involved in blood sugar metabolism and energy maintenance; plays a role in metabolism of calcium and vitamin C; involved in structuring of basic genetic material (DNA and RNA)." It is found in apples, cherries, broccoli, carrots, beans, potatoes, chicken, turkey, milk, wheat bread, barley, brown rice, dates, spinach, sunflower seeds, and walnuts.

POTASSIUM is important for normal functioning of muscles and nerves. *The following quote regarding potassium is from "2001 Current Medical Diagnosis & Treatment" by Lawrence M. Tierney, Jr., Stephen J. McPhee, and Maxine A. Papadakis. "It is involved in healthy, steady functioning of the nervous system; supports the heart, muscles, kidneys, blood."* Potassium helps keep a normal heart rhythm. It is found in apples, melons, onions, wheat, rice, apricots, berries, cherries, grapes, oranges, pears, broccoli, carrots, tomatoes, beans, potatoes, chicken, turkey, milk, avocados, barley, beets, brown rice, brussel sprouts, cauliflower, corn, dates, figs, nectarines, raisins, sunflower seeds, and walnuts.

PHOSPHORUS adds strength. Information regarding phosphorus is recorded in "2001 Current Medical Diagnosis & Treatment" by Lawrence M. Tierney, Jr., Stephen J. McPhee, and Maxine A. Papadakis. "It is involved in bone and tooth formation, cell growth and repair, energy maintenance, heart contraction, kidney function, healthy activity of nerves and muscles, the body's use of vitamins." It is found in apples, wheat, corn, rice, orange, broccoli, carrots, beans, chicken, and milk.

IRON is the #1 deficiency in the U. S. "Iron supports growth and development in children; involved in the production of hemoglobin; helps build resistance to disease." This quote is from "2001 Current Medical Diagnosis & Treatment" by Lawrence M. Tierney, Jr., Stephen J. McPhee, and Maxine A. Papadakis. Iron is an element of the oxygen carrying pigment of red blood cells. It can be found in apples, corn, rice, cherries, carrots, beans, potatoes, whole grain cereal, nuts, chicken, turkey, beef, liver, pinto beans, raisins, sunflower seeds, eggs, fish, spinach, and raisins.

ZINC. "Zinc promotes burn and wound healing; supports the immune system; involved in carbohydrate and protein digestion; plays a role in reproductive organ growth and development." This quote comes from "2001 Current Medical Diagnosis & Treatment" by Lawrence M. Tierney, Jr., Stephen J. McPhee and Maxine A. Papadakis. It is found in grapes, broccoli, tomatoes, beans, potatoes, chicken, turkey, brown rice, oats, brewers yeast, liver, seafood, bran, peas, spinach, and carrots.

VITAMIN A helps prevent cancer and is very important for good eyesight. It is necessary for normal growth and fights against infection. The following quote is also from "2001 Current Medical Diagnosis & Treatment" by Lawrence M. Tierney, Jr., Stephen J. McPhee and Maxine A. Papadakis. "It strengthens mucous membranes, the immune system, adrenal glands and eyes." It is found in apples, melons, corn, apricots, berries, cherries, grapes, oranges, pears, broccoli, carrots, chicken, liver, milk, yellow, orange, and red fruits, dairy products, margarine, fish-liver oil, yellow vegetables, egg yolk, and honey.

VITAMIN B1. "It supports healthy functioning of the heart, muscles, and nerves. It plays a role in the breakdown of carbohydrates, and helps maintain normal enzyme function." This is another informative quote from "2001 Current Medical Diagnosis & Treatment" by Lawrence M. Tierney, Jr., Stephen J. McPhee, and Maxine A. Papadakis. It is found in onions, wheat, corn, rice, apricots, grapes, pears, broccoli, beans, turkey, milk, wheat foods, bran, wheat germ, baked potatoes, avocados, yogurt, raw peanuts, Canadian bacon, watermelon, ham, and green peas. Thiamin, vitamin B1, is a water-soluble vitamin. From the same book, this quote is also taken. "The primary role of thiamin is as precursor of thiamin pyrophosphate, a coenzyme required for several important biochemical reactions necessary for carbohydrate oxidation. Thiamin is also thought to have an independent role in nerve conduction in peripheral nerves."

VITAMIN B12 helps you to not become anemic. "It is involved in growth and development; involved in production of red blood cells; helps the body use folic acid; supports healthy functioning of the nervous system." This quote was found in "2001 Current Medical Diagnosis & Treatment" by Lawrence M. Tierney, Jr., Stephen J. McPhee, and Maxine A. Papadakis. Vitamin B12 is found in fortified cereals, bran cereal, oat flakes, wheat flakes, skim or whole milk, chicken, ricotta cheese, roast, steak, pork, chicken, and fish.

VITAMIN B6 helps prevent osteoporosis. The following two quotes are from "2001 Current Medical Diagnosis & Treatment" by Lawrence M. Tierney, Jr., Stephen J. McPhee, and Maxine A. Papadakis. and regard Vitamin B6. "Vitamin B6 deficiency most commonly occurs as a result of interactions with medications - especially isoniazid, cycloserine, penicillamine, and oral contraceptives - or of alcoholism. ... Vitamin B6 deficiency can be effectively treated with oral vitamin B6 supplements." It is found in bananas, barley, and brussel sprouts.

VITAMIN C helps prevent cancer. So much is known about Vitamin C, but it is always interesting to learn more about this wonderful vitamin. The following quote is taken from "2001 Current Medical Diagnosis & Treatment" by Lawrence M. Tierney,

Jr., Stephen J. McPhee, and Maxine A. Papadakis. "Vitamin C is a potent antioxidant involved in many oxidation-reduction reactions and is also required for the synthesis of collagen. It increases the absorption of inonheme iron and is involved in tyrosine metabolism, wound healing, and drug metabolism. ... Most cases of Vitamin C deficiency seen in the USA are due to dietary inadequacy in the urban poor, the elderly, and chronic alcoholics. Patients with chronic illnesses such as cancer and chronic renal failure and individuals who smoke cigarettes are also at risk." It helps maintain strong bones, and teeth, and helps iron absorption. It is found in apples, melons, onions, corn, berries, cherries, grapes, pears, broccoli, green vegetables, carrots, tomatoes, potatoes, apricots, blueberries, cabbage, cauliflower, cranberry juice, orange juice, strawberries, sweet potatoes, and watermelon.

VITAMIN D Used in the treatment for chronic hypoparathyroidism. It is also important for strong bones and teeth and aids in calcium absorption. It is found in fortified cereals, margarine, milk, egg yolks, liver, tuna, halibut and sunlight.

VITAMIN E helps prevent heart disease. It helps to form red blood cells and slows down aging. The following quote comes from "2001 Current Medical Diagnosis & Treatment" by Lawrence M. Tierney, Jr., Stephen J. McPhee, and Maxine A. Papadakis. "Vitamin E, like B-caotene and vitamin C, may also play a role in protection against cancer, coronary heart disease, and cataracts through its antioxidant function. ...Clinical deficiency of vitamin E is most commonly due to severe malabsorption, the genetic disorder abetalipoproteinemia, or, in children with chronic cholestatic liver disease, biliary artesia or cystic fibrosis." It is found in wheat, rice, honey, orange juice, vegetable oils, nuts, meat, green vegetables, cereals and sunflower seeds.

VITAMIN K helps to build bones strong. It is very important because it promotes blood clotting. Another quote from "2001 Current Medical Diagnosis & Treatment" by Lawrence M. Tierney, Jr., Stephen J. McPhee, and Maxine A. Papadakis, regarding this vitamin follows. "Vitamin K plays a role in coagulation by acting as a cofactor for the posttranslational y-carboxylation of zymogens II, VII, IX, and X. ... Without y-carboxylation, these reactions on the platelet surface occur slowly and hemostasis is impaired. ... Vitamin K is supplied in the diet primarily in leafy vegetables and endogenously from synthesis by intestinal bacteria. Factors that contribute to Vitamin K deficiency include poor diet, malabsorption, and broad-spectrum antibiotics suppressing colonic flora." It is also found in cheese, pork, liver, yogurt, and apricots.

Doctors always stress **fiber** as an important part of diet. It is found in raisins, raspberries, spinach, strawberries, apples, apricots, barley, beets, blueberries, cereal, broccoli, brown rice, cherries, corn, dates, figs, oats, oatmeal, pears, pinto beans, white potatoes, prunes, and pumpkin.

STRAWBERRIES help boot memory, and slows brain aging.

FISH fight heat disease, depression, and lowers blood pressure.

PURPLE GRAPE JUICE fights cancer, prevents osteoporosis, and fights heart disease

CRANBERRY JUICE fights urinary tract infections.

OATS lowers blood cholesterol, and reduces heart disease.

BANANAS help the body to use energy better, helps prevent osteoporosis.

Become a good label reader. Fats have 9 calories per gram. Carbohydrates have 4 calories per gram. Protein has 4 calories per gram. The elder you are helping should see a doctor or dietitian before anything is changed from their diet. Find out from their doctor what their calorie, fat, cholesterol, and carbohydrate regulations are, if any. Check to make sure the medicines they are taking don't require food restrictions. If they do, change the diet accordingly. You can give them a healthy diet, but you can't force them to eat it. They are all individuals whatever their circumstance is; still living alone, in an assisted living area, an adult family home, hospital, or nursing home.

A caution: even though these foods, vitamins, and hints have been given, sometimes illnesses strike no matter what the diet is. Nevertheless, they do help for many people to keep them healthier. Following is a chart showing medicine abbreviations you'll see on medicine bottles. Double check with this listing if you've forgotten the doctor's exact instructions. Specific information regarding measurements and abbreviations comes from "2001 Current Medical Diagnosis & Treatment" by Lawrence M. Tierney, Jr., Stephen J. McPhee, and Maxine A. Papadakis.

"Medication Categories and Abbreviations

TIMES

Term	Abbreviation
before meals	ac
twice a day	BID
at bed time	hs
after meals	P.C.
when necessary	PRN
as needed	PRN
every	q
every day	Q.D.
every hour	qlh
every 4 hours	q4
four times a day	qid
every other day	qod
immediately	STAT
three times a day	TID

right ear	ad
left ear	as
both ears	au
intramuscular	I.M.
intravenous	I.V.
by or through	per
by mouth	po
by way of rectum	pr
subcutaneous	sq

AMOUNT

Measurement

Term	Abbreviation
cubic centimeter (also milliliter)	cc
gram	gm or GM
grain	gr
drop	gtt
one (1)	+
two (2)	++
milligram	mg
hmicrogram	mcg
one-half	ss

OTHER

Term	Abbreviation
with	c
capsule	cap.
cream	cr
tablet	tab.
ointment	ung.
without	s
sig	label
ss	one-half
tab	tablet

by way of vagina	pv
right eye	od

left eye ....os		both eyes ....ou	
Term	Abbreviation	Term	Abbreviation
1000 ml =..............1 quart		milliliters/ centimeters =f ....luid	
30 ml =..................2 Tablespoonfuls = 1 oz.		grams = ...solid	
30 gm =..................1 ounce		60 mg = ...1 grain	
1 tbsp = ...1/2 fluid ounce		1 tsp = ...5 cc	
3 tsp = ...1 tablespoonful		*per...........................by or through*	
po...........................by mouth		*as..............................left ear*	
au.........................both ears		*44"*	

Help is often needed to keep your relative or client clean. If they are in another living situation, you probably won't need to worry about this, because it should be done by staff. But if they are staying in your home, here are a few warnings and information regarding bathing. Often times, they hate the idea of getting wet at all, so it can be a real challenge for all involved. Always encourage them to wash their hands when you are helping them in the bathroom in the morning to freshen up and brush their hair. For bathing, an adapted shower stall seat may be a safer option if they are limited in mobility. If they are in a wheelchair, a chair can be obtained that is wheeled in and out of the shower. It is important to also have handrails and a nonslip mat at the floor for safety. You can help further by having all the needed toiletries out and ready for use. Make sure the water is not too hot. Pass the shower head to them to use if they are still able. In this way, they don't feel like every part of their life is being taken away from them. If they desire a bath, seek the help of a health professional who may suggest the use of special equipment. If they are unable to get out of bed safely, a bedbath is needed. When doing this, cover up as much of their body as possible as you wash the part you are working on. This will stop them from becoming chilled. If they are bedridden, you can get a hair washing tray to use for washing, or powder washes that can be purchased at any drug store.

If and when you are working as a caregiver, you may feel many losses, on a personal level. This doesn't include the feelings you develop with family or patients, but for yourself. When these feelings come along, you need to step back, acknowledge them, and make changes so they don't affect or disrupt the work you are doing now. There is the frustrations at loss of time for yourself. When this happens, have other workers take over on a permanent part time basis so you have some breathing room for your own self. If you don't have other workers, it is time for you to start hiring so you will have the needed relief. When working at hospitals, or day and night shifts at nursing homes, adult family homes, or adult day centers, you'll get away unless you are an owner. Still, when taking care of people that need your help, you will often need more than one person to work with. Taking time away will bring you the relief you need.

Are you the only caregiver? Are you taking care of a mom or dad, or other relative with no help? You need to express yourself to family at this time of need and work out other arrangements. These are people that need our help at all times. You can't be awake and alert to help them twenty-four hours a day, seven day a week. You need help, and you must let family or your employer know when you start to become too overloaded. Do you feel guilty that your loved one is somewhere else instead of in your home? Depending upon circumstances, this is often the case. There is nothing to feel guilty about. It may be hard, but try to accept the fact that they need more help than you can give at this time. Visiting them, showing your love will tighten their relationship with you. No doubt at the time they need help, you are busy working outside of the home, busy raising your own children, or cannot physically do the work needed yourself. Don't feel guilty. Have the rest of your family help. If you are an only child, have friends help if they desire. Often times, when people are ill , it is too disruptive to be in that atmosphere in your home all of the time, along with the rest of your family; spouse and children. You need to find another place. Sometimes, it works out wonderfully for your family member to stay in your home until they pass on, other times it doesn't. Don't feel guilty. Your loved one will get the care they need if you are diligent in finding the correct place for them. This time of change can be a great time of stress for you also. As a relative, you may feel stress that you are not doing the complete package. Don't feel guilty about this, because in most cases, it is impossible for children or other relatives to take complete care of the needy loved one. Realize that time brings changes. Hopefully, you will have learned that lesson earlier in life.

Sometimes changes are good, sometimes not. That is life. How are you dealing with the changes? When the stress is too great, turn to friends, family, senior centers, hospitals, and churches for information and help. Any of these sources may be a great help to you. You just need to ask. When you have reached the decision of placement, much stress will leave you immediately.

How are you, as the caregiver, or as the power of attorney feeling? Do you have any health needs and concerns yourself? It may be hard to tend to them when you're busy helping someone else much worse, but you need to. Hire another caregiver while you go have a check up. If you are not healthy, you can't be a big help for others.

Being a caregiver, in whatever spectrum of job it is, can be very taxing. If you're working in hospitals, nursing homes, assisted living, adult family homes or another care facility, you may at times feel shame. Don't let these feelings stop you in the proper care of the person you are trying to help. You may feel humiliation, disgrace, or embarrassment. How do you think the ill person feels? No doubt, often the same. Instead of using degrading remarks, encourage and try to uplift their spirits. When it is a very low point in their life, just standing by and holding their hand will help them not to feel so lost, so abandoned. Don't feel shame towards the patient, but toward people who cannot accept the reality of their loved one.

People who are ill often feel isolated. Often their caregivers feel it too. Again, that is why it is important to get out of the atmosphere of the ill as often as possible. As a caregiver, you can't help or uplift them if you are constantly downhearted yourself. If it is your parents you are caring for, often you may feel the situation has been turned around, and you are parenting them. To a certain extent, you are. This is important for both of you, but not if it causes a great chasm between you. Get the help you need by bringing in extra help, or placing them in a residence where they will have full time care. Are you getting the help you need?

CHAPTER SIX

Cost Concerns

11 "I guide you in the way of wisdom and lead you along straight paths.
12 When you walk, your steps will not be hampered; when you run, you will not stumble.
13 Hold on to instruction, do not let it go; guard it well, for it is your life." Proverbs 4:11-13

"**G**od is able to make all grace abound toward you, that you always have all sufficiency in all things, may have an abundance for every good work." 2 Corinthians 9:8. For your own personal benefit, try and follow a few of these money handling hints. Your concern for finances can be a stumbling block for your faith, or a stepping stone. God will guide your steps and provide for you, even when it seems the roof has fallen through for you. Count your blessings, and you'll see how truly rich you are. Seek out advice from a financial advisor for your loved one and stick to the disciplined savings plan suggested. To stay vital, explore new hobbies or take a vacation. You'll gain so much more when you invest life with learning experiences. Try and keep your loved one's money free of debt and balance their investments. I know you are concerned about paying for your elders needs, but try and keep a light heart about it. John D. Rockefeller said, "I have made many millions, but they have brought me no happiness. I would barter them all for the days I sat on an office stand in Cleveland and counted myself rich on three dollars a week."

When you or your family collectively have decided your parents or other loved ones need more help than where they are living alone, shop around. Find out from their doctor and visits you have with them what is really needed. Do they only need assisted living, visiting workers, adult family homes, a full nursing home, or a psychiatric hospital?

From there, check out the places in your area that would fulfill their needs and price them out. How many in your family are able to contribute financial help if the elderly do not have enough money to meet their needs? Get a family member with the gift of numbers to help. They would most like be named the Power of Attorney, if one has not already been chosen to do this. Have your attorney draw up the paperwork for this so there are no questions later.

Visit the specific places for your loved one that would meet their needs. Have in mind what your family can afford before you even start to look. Visit as many places as you can to get a good feel of what is offered, and you will end up with a few favorites to choose from.

If you are the power of attorney, double check to see if the loved one has a pension (civil service, carpenter's, veteran's, teacher's, etc.). Are there any nontaxable holdings? How about a money market account? Are they receiving social security? Are there any annuities, or certificate of deposits? What is the balance of their checking and savings account? Check their most recent state and federal tax returns to figure their yearly income. You'll feel like a snoop when you do this, but it definitely needs to be done. Are they getting medicare yet?

Contact DSHS in your state to find out how they can help. If there are financial difficulties right from the beginning, they usually can give a great deal of information to guide a great deal. Be fore-warned, there is usually a lot of paperwork to fill out, but that is common for insurances and/or state papers. They deal with so many people, paperwork becomes the avenue they use to achieve the goal. DSHS can help from the start if that is needed financially, or help direct you into other proper directions if your family is financially able to take care of the elder. They can send out lists of places for you to consider. Contact the elder's insurance to see how much, if any, they will help the elder you are concerned about. Sometimes there is no coverage, other times, a lot. Help your elder out by calling the insurance company and getting the specifics down for you and your family to have knowledge about. Contact the city to see what programs they have set up to help the elderly. Call the Red Cross for help. A lot of times, volunteers from the Red Cross can help with transportation and shopping. If possible, visit a senior center in your city , and find out the wealth of information and help they can often provide for you. Are there any churches or service organizations in your city that are especially drawn to helping the elderly? Contact them for help and information. You can also contact community mental health centers, family service agencies, home care agencies, hospitals, nursing schools. Also, check into the United Way, Department of Veteran's Affairs, unions and retiree organizations, and the National Council on the Aging. The address for the National Council on the Aging, Inc is: 600 Maryland Ave. SW, West Wing 100, Washington D.C. 20024.

Contact agencies specializing in the disease your elder has. They can be a great resource also.In this way, you don't have to feel so overwhelmed. It is a daunting task at the beginning if you let it be. Instead, go over what has just been read, write down your goals for the day, week, month, and go from there. Consider investing in an HMO if you have one in the area. The monthly premium may be less than what is being paid out now.

Who do you need to contact? Who do you need to call? What places do you need to visit? You don't have to accomplish everything in the first hour or day. Set it out on your calendar. Call relatives or friends to help go along with you. When you have a plan to follow, the hard task of moving will become easier.A valid concern for elders and children alike is the cost of health care. Medicare (a limited federal convalescent health insurance program) only pays 2% of the total dollars spent on nursing home care. You must be 65 to receive Medicare. After the client pays the first hospital bill of up to $592, Medicare will pay the hospital charges for the next 60 days. From day 61 to day 90, the patient will pay $148 a day. From the 91st day to 150th day, the patient will pay $296 a day.

Medicaid is a cooperative federal state assistance program. It is care services for low income people. It is limited to low income, the blind, the disabled, and others who receive public assistance. It pays for nursing home care, in certified homes and qualified people. Don't be afraid to apply for it if you think it will help. Our tax money pays for this.

Information regarding Alzheimers disease and money follows in the following quote from "Textbook of Anatomy & Physiology" by Catherine Parker Anthony, R. N., B. A., M. S., and Norma Jane Kolthoff, R. N., B. S., Ph. D.. "Another major concern is managing the income and financial assets of the person with Alzheimers disease. People in the early stages usually give up quite readily the complex tasks associated with handling money. ... People with Alzheimer's may be at risk of financial exploitation by family members, friends, brokers, telemarketers, and other salespeople. " If you know someone with Alzheimer's is living alone, you should notify the family or even help the person yourself if possible to make sure bills are paid on time. If you are the Power of Attorney, arrange for the bills to be sent to your home. Permission from the aged is necessary for this, but if you can share the legitimate concerns, hopefully they will agree to this and be protected. Social security checks and other income can be protected by electronic transfers to the bank. To cut down on telephone solicitations to the patient's home, send their name, address, and telephone number to: Telephone Preference Service, P.O. Box 9014, Farmingdale, NY 11735. If you suspect the elderly you are caring for is the victim of fraud, contact the local office of the state's attorney and the National Fraud Information Center at (800) 876-7060. Ask for the booklet "Rising Cost of Care".

Insurance reimbursements often fall short of actual costs. That is why it is so important to have two insurances. One is Life Insurance and the second one Private Health Insurance. Medicare or Medicaid does not pay the bills completely, and these insurances should fill in and cover what is not paid for from the government. Families pay for the indirect costs of caregiving, too - food, notions, postage, transportation, and more. The result? The family budget is stretched to the maximum or falls short. This is why it is so important to have the elderly covered by these two insurances. In Washington state, elders can contact S. H. I. B. A. (Senior Health Insurance Benefit Advisors). These volunteer advisors will answer your insurance questions, and offer help in programs to give you more information.

If a will has not been made, and your parent is mentally able to do this, contact a lawyer and get a will started. When it has been made, make sure you know where it is kept, who drew it up, the attorney's name if needed, the name of the executor, and if there is a separate letter detailing the handing out of personal items, such as heirlooms, and where they are kept.

From "The Help, Hope And Cope Book For People With Aging Parents" by Patricia H. Rushford, I found she gave a number of good hints regarding insurance. Double check your parent's current policy and replace or up-date if necessary. Here are some pitfalls to avoid in choosing a health insurance policy to cover an aging parent.

"1. Be careful about obtaining a policy with a preexisting illness exclusion. This means that if you have and are being treated for a particular illness, the policy will not cover you if you need medical attention for that problem for a defined period of time. Many policies stipulate a three-month exclusion, some six months, and some longer. While a three month exclusion may be satisfactory, policies with no preexisting illness exclusions would be preferable.

2. Beware of policies that advertise, "No medical examination required." These usually have a long preexisting condition exclusion. They not only don't examine the policy holder, they may not pay either.

3. Don't trust a policy simply because it was recommended by a friend or a reputable organization. Check out the terms of the policy and whether or not it meets your parent's needs.

4. Most likely, you will only need one health insurance policy. Look with suspicion on an agent who tries to sell you more than you need.

5. Some insurance policies cover home health care and skilled nursing home expenses, but few, if any, cover intermediate or custodial care.

6. Beware the policy that sets a low limit on the total number of days for hospital coverage or amount paid per year, or that excludes payment for the first few days of hospitalization. Sometimes the monthly payments promised may seem impressive, but when you actually consider hospital costs and the average length of stay you find it covers you about as adequately as a fig leaf.

7. Don't purchase a policy that permits the insurance company to cancel if claims are too high. Your parents should have the right to review the policy every year.

8. Be wary of "limited offers." It isn't necessary to rush into any insurance policy, If it's here today and gone tomorrow, you know it wasn't for you anyway. However, time limits base on age may be legitimate.

9. Most reputable firms allow the consumer a ten to thirty day period to examine an insurance policy. If, before the end of that trial period, you decide not to take it, the money must be refunded. Make certain this trial period is available.

10. Premium payments should be made by check or money order so you have a receipt. Never pay cash and never make the check out to the agent - only to the insurance company."

"I'm afraid we'll be broke," a worried caregiver told me. This fear is well founded. An Associated Press article, published in the Physicians Financial News in October 1994, says it costs $213,000 to care for one patient. In the article, Edward Truschke, president of the Alzheimer's Association, is quoted as saying, "The disease is draining the resources of this country and its citizens at a greater rate than we thought."

Nobody can accurately predict how long an Alzheimer's patient will live. The patient could be in a nursing home for 8 to 10 years, and costs are rising. Many families are troubled with costs long after the death.

Visit with your financial broker if you have one, for more information and help. He can give you information on the tax laws and how to safely transfer your money into safer accounts. Talk to your friends who have elderly parents or loved ones also. What are they doing? Have they found anything to help you?

I hesitated to give you this information, but feel it is important for you to know everything, good and bad, about all of the possible diseases and financial problems your elder may encounter. Not everyone will suffer from them, but it is important for the reader to know about all of the negative possibilities. From there, you can, with your family, work towards positive outcomes. You all need to be in agreement with and happy with the new residence for your elder and the price or there will be problems. Try to work out the concerns before a move is made. That way, the elder can be moved more easily and you can be at rest in this big decision.. Have you found the special place yet?

CHAPTER SEVEN

Finding the Right Doctor

The following two quotes were found in "14,000 Quips & Quotes" by E. C. McKenzie. In this book, I have covered many concerns of getting older. We also need humor, even when it seems it can't be found. "Old age is when most of the names in your little black book are doctors." I couldn't resist because it seems the truth so often with older people. This is another quote from the same book, "Medical doctors measure physical health by how the tongue looks. The Great Physician measures spiritual health by how the tongue acts." But it can be frustrating trying to find the right doctor, right? You want a doctor who will treat your relative or other loved one with respect, love, and the latest medical knowledge concerning their illness. Hard to find?

A. Since you have become more aware of the different dementias and illnesses of the elderly, you can ask the doctor your elderly one is going to if they have special training or awareness of this. If not, find a doctor or clinic that does have the knowledge. This will take work on your part perhaps, but will be well worth it. Although there are not many, try to find a doctor with geriatrics training and certification. Other health professionals can help you too. Try and find a doctor that will communicate to you, as well as your relative, in words that you can understand. Medical jargon is okay with staff, but frustrating for the normal Joe to understand at serious and momentous times as these.

Getting the right doctor will make your loved one's life a lot easier, and yours too. Many medicines can help the different illnesses, but if the doctor is not aware of them, they can't help. A doctor having knowledge regarding the elderly can help you accept the limitations more easily if they can talk to you in a knowledgeable manner that will give you understanding.

If possible, find friends you can unload your worries upon. Ones who will be helpful to you. Sometimes, at the worst possible time, your best friend is not home. Keep on until you find another caring friend. Sometimes it is hard to wait, or to live through momentous decisions that need to be made.

When you are aware changes are going on, get the concerned person to visit the doctor. Important points to remember and learn from the doctor are found in "2001 Current Medical Diagnosis & Treatment" by Lawrence M. Tierney, Jr., Stephen J. McPhee, and Maxine A. Papadakis. With a thorough examination the doctor can discover:

"1. The exact nature of the person's illness,
2. whether or not the condition can be reversed or treated
3. the nature and extent of the disability
4. the areas in which the person can still function successfully,
5. whether the person has other health problems that need treatment and that might be making her mental problems worse,
6. the social and psychological needs and resources of the sick person and the family or caregiver, and
7. the changes you can expect in the future."

In order to help the client, you must accept the diagnosis. If you have doubts, get a 2nd and 3rd diagnosis. This important truth is verified from "2001 Current Medical Diagnosis & Treatment" by Lawrence M. Tierney, Jr., Stephen J. McPhee, and Maxine A. Papadakis. "Denial is often reinforced by the misleading or seemingly absent symptoms of the disease. After all, the person with Alzheimer's Disease may appear physically healthy. ... The fluctuating nature of the symptoms can also make you wonder about the diagnosis. "

It is important for you, or the caregiver, to keep close records and charts on the ill. Then you can take these with you when you go to the doctor. Has new medicine affected their sleeping or eating habits? How? Let the doctor know. Sometimes, it will take two to three weeks for a new medicine to be affective on a person. Find out if there are other reactions you should be looking for. What are the side affects of the new medicine? Everyone reacts differently, so it may take a little while to discover the answers to these questions. Ask their doctor to please double check the medicines. Will the new medicine react badly to a current medicine they are taking? If so, something needs to be changed. Find out beforehand if this is a possibility, and monitor the client's actions closely to report back to the doctor. From this, they can tell if a medicine is being affective or not.

Most people sixty-five and older experience a minor loss in brain functions. This is normal. Only fifty percent decline significantly. There isn't any test to decipher between normal forgetfulness and the Alzheimer's disease. Dementia is the main term used for anything pertaining to brain failure. Alzheimer's takes many years to come to fruition. It slowly damages the brain only visible upon microscopic examination of the brain. It has only become noticeable since we have started living longer. An Alzheimer's test starts with a complete physical that assesses physical health, and other diseases that can affect thinking. A brain tumor, diabetes, and arterial disease can affect the brain, so they need to be ruled out if Alzheimer's is determined. They should also get a neurological check as part of their exam. The doctor may order a chest x-ray, CT scan (computerized tomogram), and MR. (magnetic resonance imaging) to discover if there are any other treatable diseases that may cause these problems.

When shopping for a doctor for yourself, or your loved one, you need to feel comfortable with them. Doctors are very busy, but did they give you a few minutes to explain your concerns about new circumstances? Did they appear to really listen to you? Try and find a doctor that helps you feel human, instead of a new specimen to examine. Then you can feel comfortable in expressing your concerns and fears.

B. Call senior centers for good references. The workers will often know, from observation and experience with seniors, who the best doctors for seniors are in your particular area.

C. Call State Aid for good references.

D. Call friends for good references.

Ask the doctor you choose to help your senior if they are interested in giving them a richer and fuller life, despite their limitations. Why not live life to the fullest?

CHAPTER EIGHT

When the End Is Near

"Even though I walk through the valley of the shadow of death, I will fear no evil, for you are with me; your rod and your staff, they comfort me." Psalm 23:4

As the threads of fiber are woven into clothing, so is suffering woven into our lives. You may ask, "When will I stop suffering?" The suffering ends when you meet Jesus on the other side. To a believer, this is the only hell they will experience, but for the non-believer, this is the closest they will get to heaven.

Suffering is a part of life. There is no way of getting around it. You will suffer because you live in a fallen world. Loosing a mate or other loved member of your life can be so very hard. How you handle suffering and how you go through suffering no one knows, until you go through it. Being good or bad, right or wrong, Christian or not, suffering will come. How you want to deal with it is up to you. Life is what you make it; good or bad, happy or sad. You can deny it, blame it on somebody or something else, but it still happens. You choose how you live. Life is but a breath of air, or a moment in time stacked up against the eternity the Lord gives us.

Don't worry. Suffering has nothing to do with God, but with this fallen world.

There is only one way out of suffering, and that is the hope Jesus Christ provides for us. He paid your ticket out of this world. He took the total suffering onto Himself at the cross. The final stage of life is death. It can come at any time to anyone. Just as we came into the world, we will leave it also.

How to survive the suffering you go through:

1. Expect it. We live in a fallen, sinful world that has pain and sorrow.
2. Believe it. We wonder about the uncertainty. Is there a possibility it will get better? What will it be like to breath my last breath?
3. Learn from it. Know what you are dealing with.
4. Give it to God. He is the only one to turn to. He is the one that holds the future.
5. Be filled with hope in the realization that there is a way out; there is an end to it.

Sometimes, when it seems there is no answer, we must rely on the facts - God's grace is sufficient in our suffering. With God's help and knowing He is there, we can go through pain we know is impossible for us to go through alone. We must trust God and let go of our suffering knowing that the Lord will carry us over to the other side. What are we trying to hang on to when the future has the promise of being so much better? Additionally, the Lord may be allowing troubles come upon you to prove to the world that men can serve God even if they suffer. God can use the hardships of suffering to test us, to humble us, to get our priorities right, and to discipline us. We see this in Job's life. Though Job was complaining and growing self righteous, in the end it led to his restoration. He found God faithful and compassionate. Job shows how much a man can take when his faith and life is in the Lord.

We must face death with

Dignity of self
Eternity in mind
Acceptance it will come
Truth of yourself in Jesus Christ
Heaven in view

Ron Dunn brings out 6 suggestions for helping a friend or loved one die in his book "Will God Heal Me? Faith In The Midst Of Suffering".

"1. **Assure them that they are not alone.** We are there and will be there for them. ... Sadly, the tendency today is to isolate the dying patient in hospitals, behind drawn curtains, with threatening signs, "No visitors." But no one should die alone. If the person is dying, your presence can't make him worse. You don't need to say anything. Just holding his hand says, "You are not alone. You are not forgotten."

2. **Encourage them to talk through their feelings and fears.** We need to realize the believer can maintain a steadfast hope in God and still experience great turmoil in the face of death. Helping a dying friend to open up and talk about their illness is one of the greatest gifts you can give. It isn't a lack of faith for patients to express the fears of dying, of what might happen to those left behind. They may have a desperate need to share these feelings but fear doing so will cause others to doubt their trust in the Lord. It is our duty to allow them to say such things without fear of judgment.

3. **Listen.** People often tell me, "I don't know what to say." Saying something is not the important thing. Being there with a listening ear is.

4. **Relive** the happy moments of their life ...

5. Most of all, **assure them** of God's continuing presence ...

6. **Focus** on the glories that are to come ...""

We think on a human level while God is far above us working on a spiritual level. We say to ourselves, "Lord, is this your final answer? Do you want to ask for a second opinion, or should we call a friend?" In a way, this is what Job was doing with the Lord. We see in the end that Job sees how awesome and powerful God can be. He holds the final answer. Sometimes, we get to thinking when we go through suffering and problems that God will answer us or do something good for us, but most of the time, this is not the case. God is God. He can do whatever He wants. He wants us to know He loves us and desires our love back to Him. With God's help , we can go through pain that we know is impossible for us to go through alone. We must trust Him and let go of our suffering, knowing the Lord will carry us over to the other side. When we suffer, and don't know why, we put the blame on God because it seems the logical thing to do. But, as Jesus suffered, so will we. We have victory and hope in Jesus for eternal life where there will be no more sorrow. When the pain and suffering is too much to bear, He will take us home to be with Him.

God wanted Job to draw close to Him and to show Job the meaning of faith. We see this by the passionate words of Job himself. No matter how we try, often human wisdom fails in comprehending divine purpose. God's answer is not always what we want to hear and often too vast for human intelligence to grasp.

We see this on a human level example when we tell our children they cannot do something. Over and over they ask why. We say, "because I said so and I don't have to explain why." But in being human, we sometimes give in because of pressure, guilt, and seeing them suffer. This gives us a little example of what God goes through. His way of doing things and loving us is far above what we can imagine or grasp.

The skillfulness needed for care will improve if you look after your own needs also. You need to acknowledge your own grief. This is a way to move forward, not fail. Go to healthcare professionals and draw from their experience and wisdom. How can you know everything to expect if you have never experienced it? Don't feel guilty if you are angry or frightened. These emotions are natural, but if you bottle them up, this adds more stress to you as you go through this hard time. Don't look upon yourself as being useless. Your presence with the ill provides essential support at this time of need.

You may be told of the impending death, but it is the job of the professionals involved to tell your relative or client. Be honest and discreet with them at this time. Let them talk. Don't be afraid to talk to them. Often, the sound of your voice will be soothing. Listen to them as they express their wishes, holding their hands for encouragement. Touching also expresses reassurance, affection, and soothes anxieties.

Hopefully, you have discussed with the patient their desires regarding their death. Do they want to die at home, at a hospital, at a nursing home? If they desire to be at home at the end, contact hospice and their doctor. Hospice is an organization that truly helps families when there is impending death. If the loved one or client desires to die at home, they will come into the home to tend to their needs, and instruct you how to care for the dying one properly. Hospice can really be a help to you; talking of the specific illness, finances, with emotional and spiritual needs. At other instances, the family may choose to take their loved one to a nursing home at this time. If they are being tended to at the hospital and are too ill to be moved, the hospital and hospice will try to make that last room as comfortable and relaxing as possible for the dying.

Common characteristics of grief:

Feelings: These are all feelings the dying one and you may both feel at this time of loss: Shock, numbness, sense of unreality, anger, irritability, guilt, self reproach, sadness, depression, anxiety, fear, hysteria, helplessness, vulnerability, low self esteem, loneliness, relief, feelings of being crazy, mood swings, and intensity of all feelings.

Physical Sensations: These sensations may come upon you or the ill person as they reflect on the finality of death: hollowness in the stomach, tightness in the chest and throat, dry mouth, oversensitiveness to noise, dizziness, headaches, shortness of breath, weakness in the muscles, lack of energy, fatigue, excess of nervous energy, heart pounding, heavy or empty feeling in body and limbs, hot or cold flashes, skin sensitivity, stomach and intestinal upsets, an increase in physical illnesses.

Thought Patterns: Thoughts run rampant in your mind that has become blurry with so thoughts ricocheting all around. You may feel any or all of the following feelings: disbelief, denial, anger, sense of unreality, preoccupation, confusion, lack of ability to concentrate, seeing, hearing, feeling the presence of the deceased, thoughts of self destruction, problems with decision making, acceptance. The dying person might feel angry because they are afraid of death. You and others may be angry because the loved one is dying.

Accept that anger is a natural step toward accepting the reality. Anger can be a good way to vent feelings. After going through the denial and anger patterns, the ill person can accept the reality of death. Assurance by others is needed at this time for them to be at peace.

Behaviors: Each person reacts to death differently. Don't expect to feel a certain way. When actual reality hits, you may feel completely differently. Some people don't say anything, but hold their pain in. If this happens, the pain will stay until they let it go. No one knows how they will react to death until they experience it.

Appetite and sleep disturbances, absent minded behavior, social withdrawal, avoiding reminders of the loss, dreams of the loss, searching and calling for the deceased, restlessness, sighing, crying, visiting places that are reminders of the loss, treasuring, carrying objects that belonged to the deceased, change in sexual activities, need for touch, hugs, contact with others, increased sensitivity to positive and negative attention, picking up mannerisms of the deceased, and exhibiting symptoms of the deceased's illness, may all be part of the living one's sorrow.

Social Changes: For the suffering and sorrowing, either an increased desire for support of close friends, or a withdrawal from friends and family, increased dependency on others, a need for acting "normal" around others, a need for relationships apart from those related to grief, self-absorbed (no energy for interest in others), marital difficulties, especially with the death of a child may be experienced. Role changes, role reversals, a change in social patterns and status, hypersensitivity to topics of loss, and need for rituals is also seen.

The grief cycle is something everyone goes through, although not everyone will have these feelings, or these feelings may not come in the same order::

1. Shock & Denial - "This isn't happening."
2. Anger & Guilt - "Why me?", "Why my loved one?", "If only ..."
3. Bargaining - "Please let everything be back to normal and I promise to ..."
4. Tears & Fears - "I can't stand it!", "I can't cope!"
5. Despair, Depression, & Resignation - "There is nothing to live for."
6. Adjustment & Acceptance - "I have survived most of my grief and have new strengths and understandings that have prepared me to move on to a new and different life."

The circle of sorrow never closes to make it complete. You are changed forever by your loss. You will never be the same. How you are changed depends on your attitude and determination. You may come through this time of loss withdrawn, bitter, angry, or you may come out of it with a new found depth of character and strength. What other losses have you suffered in your life? That determines how you will respond to this recent loss. We are all different and handle loss different. What was your relationship to the deceased? What were the circumstances surrounding the death? What are your current influences in this present time?

The following is a good list given "2001 Current Medical Diagnosis & Treatment" by Lawrence M. Tierney, Jr., Stephen J. McPhee, and Maxine A. Papadakis. If you have lost someone, you can realize these truths when you read through them. When helping another person in their sorrow, it is good to remember these so you can understand their situation better and help in their grieving process.

"The Grieving Person's Bill of Rights

1 . You have the right to experience your own unique grief. No

one else will grieve in exactly the same way you do. So, when you turn to others for help, don't allow them to tell what you should or should not be feeling.

2. You have the right to talk about your grief. Talking about your grief will help you heal. Seek out others who will allow you to talk as much as you want, as often as you want, about your grief.

3. You have the right to feel a multitude of emotions. Confusion, disorientation, fear, guilt and relief are just a few of the emotions you might feel as part of your grief journey. Others may try to tell you that feeling angry, for example, is wrong. Don't take these judgmental responses to heart. Instead, find listeners who will accept your feelings without condition.

4. You have the right to be tolerant of your physical and emotional limits. Your feelings of loss and sadness will probably leave you feeling fatigued. Respect what your body and mind are telling you. Get daily rest. Eat balanced meals. And don't allow others to push you into doing things you don't feel ready to do.

5. You have the right to experience grief "attacks". Sometimes, out of nowhere, a powerful surge of grief may overcome you. This can be frightening, but is normal and natural. Find someone who understands and will let you talk it out.

6. You have the right to make use of ritual. The funeral ritual does more than acknowledge the death of someone loved. It helps provide you with the support of caring people. More important, the funeral is a way for you to mourn. If others tell you that rituals such as these are silly or unnecessary, don't listen.

7. You have the right to embrace your spirituality. If faith is part of your life, express it in ways that seem appropriate to you. Allow yourself to be around people who understand and support your religious beliefs. If you feel angry at God, find someone to talk with who won't be critical of your feelings of hurt and abandonment.

8. You have the right to search for meaning. You may find yourself asking, "Why did he or she die? Why this way? Why now? Some of your questions may have answers, but some may not. And watch out for the cliched responses some people may give you. Comments like, "It was God's will" or "Think of what you have to be thankful for" are not helpful and you do not have to accept them.

9. You have the right to treasure your memories. Memories are one of the best legacies that exist after the death of someone loved. You will always remember. Instead of ignoring your memories, find others with whom you can share them.

10. You have the right to move toward your grief and heal. Reconciling your grief will not happen quickly. Remember, grief is a process, not an event. Be patient and tolerant with yourself and avoid people who are impatient and intolerant with you. Neither you nor those around you must forget that the death of someone loved changes your life forever."

As we look at the story of Joseph in the Old Testament, we can sense he didn't try to understand all the reasons why God allowed him to suffer the slavery and imprisonment. He didn't see the big picture of why he suffered until later. When he saw his brothers and father safely in Egypt with him, he knew this was God's plan. He could see how God turned his suffering into good. The world's intention of evil darkness and depression that is trying to overcome you possibly through your trying time did not stop Joseph from trusting in the Lord.

Like Joseph, try and keep your eyes on God, not your circumstances. With grief, you have the feelings of abandonment, anger, anxiety and panic, depression, disappointment, fear, frustration, grief, guilt, shame, isolation, envy, love, regret, relief, resignation or acceptance. All of these feelings sometimes feel like they are hammering at you all at the same time. Before you collapse, find a chair to sit down on. In spite of the people around you or the situation, try and relax. Remember the one that has passed on. Everyone is different in how they feel grief or show sorrow. Just be yourself, and struggle through this hard time instead of trying to live up to everyone else's expectations of you. Your sorrow is different with every grief because you are different. You change a little with the loss of each aspect of your life. You may look at these events in your life with a whole new light. Some of these avenues affected may be your mental, emotional, physical, spiritual health, or cultural influences, family dynamics, relationships, and gender.

When you are with your loved one that is dying, you may not know how to act and speak with them. Part of this is because you have started the process of letting go. If death has never happened to you with close ones before, you have no idea of where to go or who to see or what to do. Emotions overwhelm you. It feels like you are in a box you can't get out of. If possible, group together with family and/or close friends for support and understanding. Let your work and other organizations you belong to know about the circumstances. They can then be more understanding and helpful as bad days come more often. You may not expect any help necessarily from them, but they need to know your circumstances. It may be surprising the help they will end up being for you. There are family members that can't resolve their agitation with a loved one, and so are left shortchanged when death comes. They are then unable to close the door completely. Try to get the family together to express their feelings with the loved one before they become too sick to appreciate it.

If you own or work at an adult family home, assisted living home, nursing home, or hospital where the client is dying , here are some suggestions for visitors so they won't feel so awkward during their visit.:

1. Try to move beyond the appearance of the sick one. Remember him or her as they once were, despite the sad appearance. It is the illness causing this appearance. Go beyond that to the person behind the ravaged body.
2. Straighten their blankets for them. They are often unable to do so, and desire to be modest.
3. Hold their hands, and stroke their arms. This will give you and them a feeling of true contact to connect in this way.

4. Talk to them about other subjects beside their illness. Current news, politics, jokes help break up the constant bad feelings they are living with when there are no visitors.

5. Tell them what they mean to you. Tears are okay, as you share the meaning they have had for you in your life.

6. Ask them if there are any phone calls they want made.

7. Because of pain medicines, they may not be fully aware. Yet hand holding is realized and appreciated.

8. If you sense they need more pain medicine, contact the nurse.

9. If something doesn't seem right, contact the appropriate people.

10. Write a note to the ill if they are asleep when you visit.

11. If you are a friend of someone who is losing their love one, suggest you stay with the ill person one day, so they can have a break. Sitting and waiting for someone to die is very tiring and draining. Anyone who has gone through this before knows that a break will bring them a little refreshing time, possibly even the courage to go on. Don't phone constantly. The family is already overwhelmed by the sense of impending loss. It is often too much for them to take. Leaving a message phone for people who are suffering can be helpful. They can listen when they feel strong enough, and return calls as they see fit. It isn't easy to maintain good manners when their heart is breaking.

12. Listen to the thoughts of the dying one. Let them express their feelings at this time without fear of condemnation.

13. Arrange for a minister to come and help them and the family at this time, if desired.

14. Give the suffering family the gift of silence or caring attention.

If someone dies that you loved deeply, and you didn't get the chance to say good-bye, often deep despair comes upon you. Encourage that person to talk it out. Give them another way of seeing the situation. Friends need to understand that for some people, closure takes years. In remembering and recalling the deceased, there is no right or wrong way in remembering them, speaking of them. Coming to terms with death doesn't happen like a scheduled program. It usually always comes when we don't want it.

Another important aspect is covered in "2001 Current Medical Diagnosis & Treatment" by Lawrence M. Tierney, Jr., Stephen J. McPhee, and Maxine A. Papadakis. "Our mental, emotional, physical, and spiritual health are major factors in how we cope with loss. People already in crisis (facing major surgery, serious illness, or complicated pregnancy, for example) may choose to postpone their mourning until their condition has stabilized. Under certain circumstances, the bereaved may never reach a state conducive to adapting. Appearances, however, are not always accurate barometers, ..."

The Book of Job shows and tells us about a man of faith in the midst of suffering. The pain of suffering can bring out words of confession we don't even understand why we speak. This suffering and pain will never be understood by us, but the Lord is there, and as Job said in Chapter 42, God's plans and reasons will persevere. The suffering may be due to a divine purpose which passes our understanding. We all will go through peaks and valleys as we live this side of heaven.

More information regarding grief is detailed in "Behaviors In Dementia" by Mary Kaplan and Stephanie B. Hoffman. "When grief is acute, emotions are raw. Mourners are often trying to just make it through the day on their feet. "If you encounter other bereaved individuals," we advise at our support groups, "do not walk up and ask about their loss. If you see someone at a restaurant, that person may just want to eat their lunch and not be reminded of her grief. Greet any bereaved individual as you normally would, 'Hello ... How are you?' and let that person determine the direction of the conversation."

How do you talk to the person in mourning? I've been in mourning myself, with my mother, my in laws, a brother in law in addition to beloved clients in my adult family home who passed away.

I have been lucky enough to have friends who allowed me to mourn my loss, whether it was from personal injury, or from the loss of a loved one. Instead of finding the correct words to share, I have found meaningful passages from books I've read. The next three quotes are from "Behaviors In Dementia" by Mary Kaplan and Stephanie B. Hoffman. "In sum, communication problems are less likely to occur when sympathy is offered at the appropriate place and time, and when the statements coordinate with the survivor's process. Sensitivity is the key for interacting with the bereaved." "Simplicity is the key to good taste, that certainly applies to giving sympathy. Simplicity and a quiet presence can bring tremendous comfort. Survivors long remember friends who sat beside them, allowing them to mourn." "...Healthy grief has a function. It allows survivors to identify, acknowledge, feel, and integrate what they love but are now without. Unhealthy grief prolongs suffering, interrupts normal activities, or prevents life from being lived to the fullest. ...Healthy grief has a flow, a natural continuing process, although that flow can include stopping to rest, reenergize, or take stock. Fixated grief, however, causes survivors to remain stuck at one point."

Trauma is coped with by 1. denial 2. unconscious denial 3. reversibility of the loss (temporary) 4. mementos 5. assuming the characteristics of the deceased 6. reproduced medical symptoms 7. searching for the deceased 8. mistaking others 9. emotions in disguise 10. anniversary reactions 11. replicated loss.

Yes, adjusting to the loss can be quite hard. The five stages of grief introduced by Elizabeth Kubler-Ross from her book "On Death and Dying" are:

1. denial,
2. anger,
3. bargaining,
4. depression, and
5. acceptance.

Grieving people can feel these emotions at any time - the stages can be felt in different order. Any of these feelings may coexist with other states, be completely skipped, occur intermittently, or repeat themselves. In Worden's grief theory, he has you go through four tasks.

1. The mourner accepts the reality of the loss - that death is permanent and irreversible.
2. Discovering how to make it through the emotional pain.
3. Adjust to the environment.
4. Move ahead. The mourner acknowledges the loss and moves into the next stage of life. The grief can easily last in the transition to new life after death of a loved one from four to six years. Grief brings us back to the reality that we are all human. It makes us recall the one that has passed on and remember the love and realize the differences that made them the individual they were. You can become more sensitive to others who need it if you have experienced it yourself.

When the golden years become the twilight zone, it is hard to understand, and sometimes, you won't. It's hard to see and hear your loved one in this condition. They say and do things that are hurtful and mean. You've got to know they don't say and do these things to hurt you, because they are out there in the twilight zone. They come in and out of the twilight zone to their real world sporadically. As their condition of aging gets worse, it's hard for them to find their way back to the real world.

If you have never been with a person who has died before, it can be frightening. The following will give you an idea of what to expect, and how to give comfort to your loved one who is dying."Many changes occur as we approach death. The changes are usually natural and expected but also can seem very different and can be frightening. ... Feel free to discuss any concerns you have with your nurse or physician. The symptoms described are how the body prepares itself for the final stages of life. "The previous quote and the following are found in the "Hospice Notebook" by Highline Homecare Services.

"1. Amount of time sleeping increases. The person may be difficult to awaken at times. (Plan conversation time for when the person seems most alert. Allow them to sleep as needed).
2. The desire to eat decreases. (Offer small servings of a

favorite food or drink being careful not to make food an issue.)

3. There may be increased confusion or forgetfulness about time, place and who people are. Speech may be difficult. (Talk calmly and gently; avoid startling or frightening the person. Remind the person where they are, who is with them and what day it is.)

4. Restlessness, pulling at bed linen or having visions of persons or things not present. (Provide reassurance, create a safe environment while trying to avoid physical restriction of person when possible.)

5. Slight decreases in person's vision and hearing. (Maintain light in room. Never assume person cannot hear you.)

6. Loss of control of urine and bowel is sometimes a problem. If needed, a urinary catheter may be used. (Place pads under person for protection and ask the Hospice nurse for guidance.)

7. Breathing patterns may change to an irregular rhythm. There may be 10-30 second periods of no breathing. Cheeks may become limp, moving in and out with each breath.

8. Secretions may increase and collect at the back of the mouth. Inability to clear the throat and remove the saliva may lead to a congestion or rattle. This is generally not uncomfortable to the person. (Turn the person on their side, or try elevating the head of the bed. Talk to the Hospice nurse who may be able to offer suggestions.)

9. As circulation slows there may be temperature and color changes. The body trunk may be warmer than usual and the legs and arms may become cool and pale. (Keep warm blankets on; do not use an electric blanket.)

10. Other comfort measures: Learn to "be with" the person without talking. Offer support through your touch and presence. For dry mouth, use Vaseline on lips and swab mouth with water or saline (salt dissolved in water). Ice chips or sucking on a moist washcloth can help dry mouth. Gently tooth brushing and good oral hygiene is

helpful. A moist washcloth on the forehead may be sooth-ing. Eye drops may help to soothe the eyes. Slight twitch-ing or muscle spasms may occur, if troublesome, ask the Hospice nurse. Turning and repositioning may be comforting, as can be a gentler backrub, handrub, or fresh powder on skin."

You, as a loved one, need help and prayers from people in deal-ing with your loved one. You are no good for your loved one if you are run down too. You get hurt quicker and say unwanted things to the loved one you are taking care of. You make bad decisions and judgments. So when your loved one is nearing death, you need to:

1. Get support - from family and friends.
2. Get good rest to build up your strength.
3. Be in God's word and pray.
4. Find a support group and read material about your loved one's condition.
5. You've got to know your loved one loves you and you're doing your best.

When your loved one is in the twilight zone, they talk about things off the wall. You wonder why they are thinking that. They bring up things from the past settled long ago, but in their own mind, they are living it over again. It is present day troubles for them. To help a person in this condition, you must limit the TV programs that are violent. Also, you can do the things they love and enjoy doing. Reading them a book and/or listening to music they like might be an option..

Have pictures in the room they enjoy seeing, or just spend time holding hands and smiling at them.

When the end is near, you need to settle all their accounts and tie up all loose ends with the loved one. You've got to feel at peace with yourself and with them. When they pass away, it is too late, so say it now. If they are Christian, you have the eternal hope you will see them again. What a promise we have in Jesus Christ, a hope of eternal life. They pass from death into glory.

It is so hard to see any good when death comes. How can we make it through ourselves, in addition to encouraging others. The quotes found in the bible were listed in Philip Yancey's book "Where Is God When It Hurts?" Reviewing them when hard times come can truly help. "The Bible describes several ways in which suffering can be used for our good.(Unless otherwise indicated, the following Bible quotations are taken from the New International Version, Zondervan Publishing House, © 1973.)

1. Refine our faith (I Peter 1:5-7) ... "who through faith are shielded by God's power until the coming of the salvation that is ready to be revealed in the last time. In this, you greatly rejoice, though now for a little while, you may have had to suffer grief in all kinds of trials. These have come so your faith-of greater worth than gold, which perished even though refined by fire-may be proved genuine and may result in praise, glory, and honor when Jesus Christ is revealed."

2. Make us mature (James 1:2-4) "Consider it pure joy, my brothers, whenever you face trials of many kinds, because you know that the testing of your faith develops perseverance. Perseverance must finish its work so that you may be mature, and complete, not lacking anything."

3. Allow an opportunity to display the works of God (John 9:1-3) "As He went along, He saw a man blind from birth. His disciples asked him, "Rabbi, who sinned, this man or his parents, that he was born blind?" "Neither this man nor his parents sinned", said Jesus, "But this happened so that the work of God may be displayed in his life."

4. Conform us to God's image (Rom. 8:28,29) "And we know that in all things God works for the good of those who love Him, who have been called according to His purpose. For those God foreknew He also predestined to be conformed to the likeness of His Son, that He may be the firstborn among many brothers."

5. Produce in us perseverance and character (Rom. 5:1-5) ..." Therefore, since we have been justified through faith, we

have peace with God through our Lord Jesus Christ, through whom we have gained access by faith into this grace in which we now stand. And we rejoice in the hope of the glory of God. Not only so, but we also rejoice in our sufferings, because we know that suffering produces perseverance, perseverance, character; and character, hope. And hope does not disappoint us, because God has poured out His love into our hearts by the Holy Spirit, whom He has given us." (Verses in full were added by author for easier understanding and clarification.)

When your loved ones do pass away, you have the right to cry and be in grief. Also, you can take as long as you need and want. It is up to you. The listing above will seem cold and heartless to the person in profound sorrow, I know. But give it time. You've got to know they are in a better place now, and at peace. You know your loved one loved you and they were loved by you.

When my wife's mother got cancer and passed away soon after, we were all so very sad. It helped for my wife to do as has been suggested. Spend as much time as possible with the dying person. Talk to them, even when they are in a coma stage. Hold their hands, caress their cheek.

Be with family and recall times together. If possible, even laugh together. Even when you are very bothered about the finality of death, remember the times you did have with the person dying.

When they die, you have to say good bye.

If it bothers you too much to actually be with the dying person, stay away and do your grieving. Yet also try and be a comfort for those gripped with grief. You are having a hard time. They need your encouragement and understanding at this time too.

Are you angry with this dying person? Give it to the Lord. Ask Him to rid you of the anger and bad memories. You can go on with your life freer and cleaner when the anger is left behind. What are you angry about? Why? What good is it doing you to be angry still? Is it making you a better person? Is the anger stealing away the love once held for a person? If you had a bad or hard relationship with the dying one, realize the one who has died can no longer hurt you.

Remember - anger is not a healing emotion, but a crippling one.

Are you having a hard time accepting the reality of your loved one dying? Unfortunately, we do not live in a world with everlasting life. Yet. Be encouraged there can be a life everlasting when Christ is in your life. Change your outlook, and think positively toward death. What?, you yell at the page. But it is only another beginning place for the person that has died. This next quote written by Patricia H. Rushford in her book "The Help, Hope, And Cope Book For People With Aging Parents" helps you to move on to your new stage in life. Parenthesis within the quote were added by this author. "Caring for your aging parents (in whatever way: by nursing home, adult family home, assisted living, hospital, at home) may be the hardest task you've ever encountered, but it may also be the most rewarding.

Come, let us celebrate birth and death, for life cannot be lived without both." Unless otherwise indicated, Bible quotations are taken from New International Version, © 1990, Zondervan Publishing House. I Corinthians 15:54, 55. "...Death is swallowed up in victory. O death, where is thy victory? O death, where is thy sting?"

Bibliography

How To Be A People Helper, Collins, Gary R., Tyndale House Pub, Wheaton, IL, 1995

The Help, Hope and Cope Book For People With Aging Parents, Rushford, Patricia H., Fleming H. Revell Co., Old Tappan, NJ, 1985

Dementia Training from Geriatric Resources, Radium Springs, NM

Hospice Notebook, Alzheimer's Education & Training Resources from Geriatric Resources, Radium Springs. NM, 1998

Hospice Notebook, Highline HomeCare Services, 1998

Alzheimers Finding The Word - A Communication Guide For Those Who Care published by Chronimed Publ., by Harriet Hodgson, 1995

The 36-Hour Day, Nancy L. Mace, M. A., Peter V. Rabins, M. D., M. P. H., A John Hopkins Press Health Book, John Hopkins University Press, 1999

Life After Loss, Moody Jr., Raymond & Arcangel, Dianne, Harper Collins Publishers, 2001

Alzheimer's Early Stages, Daniel Kuhn, M. S. W., Hunter House, 1999

Tangled Minds, Muriel R. Gillick, M. D., Penguin Putnum Inc., 1998

Programming For Dementia, presented by Geriatric Resources, Inc., Geriatric Resources, Inc., 1994

Smart Medicine For Healthier Living, Janet Zand, LAC, OMD, Allan N. Spreen, MD, CNC, James B. Lavalle, RPh, ND, Avery Publishing Group, 1999

Current Medical Diagnosis & Treatment, edited by Lawrence M. Tierney, Jr., MD, Stephen J. McPhee, MD, Maxine A. Papadakis, MD, Lange Medical Books/McGraw-Hill, 2001

Smart Medicine For Healthier Living, by Janet Zand, LAC, OMD, Allan N. Spreen, MD, CNC, James B. LaValle, RPh, ND, Avery Publishing Group, 1999

Caregiver's Handbook, A Complete Guide To Home Health Care, VNAA , DK Publishing, Inc., 1998

Nursing Homes, The Complete Guide, Mary B. Forrest, L.P.N., Christopher B. Forrest, M.D., Richard Forrest, copyright by Facts On File, 1990

Healing Conversations, What To Say When You Don't Know What To Say, by Nance Guilmartin, Jossey-Bass, A Wiley Co. Publisher, 2002

Life Worth Living, The Eden Alternative in Action, by William H. Thomas, M.D., VanderWyk & Burnham, a Division of

Publicom, Inc., 1996

But This Is My Mother!, by Cynthia Loucks, VanderWyk & Burnham, a Division of Publicom, Inc., 2000

Sunshine Home, by Eve Bunting, Clarion Books, 1994

Groups, Process & Practice, by Marianne Schneider Corey/Gerald Corey, published by Brooks/Cole Thomson Learning Pub., 2002

14,000 Quips & Quotes, For Speakers, Writers, Editors, Preachers, and Teachers, by E. C. McKenzie, Baker Book House, 1980

The American Medical Association Family Medical Guide, editor in chief Jeffrey R. M. Kunz, M. D., Published by The Reader's Digest Association, Inc., by permission of Random House, Inc., 1982

Thoughts From Wolfelt, by Alan D. Wolfelt, Published by Batesville Management Services, 1994

Keeping Your Brain Young, by Guy McKhann, M. D. and Marilyn Albert, Ph. D., John Wiley & Sons Pub., 2002

Textbook of Anatomy & Physiology, by Catherine Parker Anthony, R. N., B. A., M. S. and Norma Jane Kolthoff, R. N., B. S., Ph. D., C. V. Mosby Co., 1971

2001 Current Medical Diagnosis & Treatment, by Lawrence M. Tierney, Jr., Stephen J. McPhee, and Maxine A. Papadakis, Lange Medical Books/McGraw-Hill Pub., 2001

Behaviors In Dementia, by Mary Kaplan & Stephanie B. Hoffman, Health Professions Press, 1998

God's Words Of Life, by Sharon Mahoe, Zondervan Corp., 1997

Where Is God When It Hurts, by Philip Yancey, Zondervan Pub. House, Grand Rapids, MI, 1977

Will God Heal Me? Faith In The Midst Of Suffering, by Ron Dunn, Multnomah Books, 1997

The Loss Of Self, by James Thomas, published by ABC-CLIO, 1987

On Death and Dying, by Elizabeth Kubler-Ross, published by MacMillan, 1969

Notes and Index

CHAPTER 1

1. Nancy L. Mace, M. A., Peter V. Rabins, M. D., M. P., **The 36 Hour Day,** (John Hopkins University Press, 1999) 1, 14, 14, 56, 60

2. Lawrence M. Tierney, Jr., Stephen J. McPhee, Maxine A. Papadakis, **2001 Current Medical Diagnosis & Treatment**, Lange Medical Books/McGraw Hill Pub., 2001, page 1082

3. Muriel R. Gillick, M. D. **Tangled Minds**, (Penguin Putnam, Inc., 1998) page 3

4. Marianne Schneider Corey and Gerald Corey, **Groups, Process & Practice,** (Brooks/Cole Thomson Learning Pub., 2002) from their book page 384,385

5. Harriet Hodgson, **Alzheimers Finding The Word - A Communication Guide For Those Who Care**, published by Chronimed Publ., 1995 from her book page 15, 16

6. Raymond Moody Jr. and Dianne Arcangel, **Life After Loss,** Harper Collins Publishers, 2001, from their book page 60

7. Alan D. Wolfelt, **Thoughts From Wolfelt**, published by Bateville Management Services, 1994, from his book, page 3

CHAPTER 2

1. Daniel Kuhn, M. S. W., **Alzheimer's Early Stages**, published by Hunter House, 1999, from his book, page 50-51

2. Muriel R. Gillick, M. D., **Tangled Minds,** published by Penguin Putnam, Inc., 1998, from her book page 53

3. Patricia H. Rushford, **The Help, Hope, and Cope Book For People With Aging Parents,** published by Fleming H. Revell Co., 1985, from her book page 143-144

4. Muriel R. Gillick, M. D., **Tangled Minds**, publisher Penguin Putnam, Inc., 1998, on bibliography and page 3

5. V.N.A.A., **Caregiver's Handbook, A Complete Guide To Home Health Care,** DK Publishing, Inc., 1998, from their book pages 9, 10.

6. William H. Thomas, M. D., **Life Worth Living, The Eden Alternative in Action,** publoished by VanderWyk & Burnham, a Division of Publicom, Inc., 1996, from his book, title page, page 9, page 44

CHAPTER THREE

1. Muriel R. Gillick, M. D., **Tangled Minds**, published by Penguin Putnam, Inc., 1998, from page 126 in her book.

2. Daniel Kuhn, M. S. W., **Alzheimer's Early Stages**, published by Hunter House, 1999, from page 99 in his book

CHAPTER FOUR

1. Gary R. Collins**, How To Be A People Helper,** published by Tyndale House Pub., 1995, from page 120 in his book

2. Nance Guilmartin, Jossey-Bass, **Healing Conversations, What To Say When You Don't Know What To Say,** A Wiley Co. Pub., 2002, page 66, 71, 72-73,

3. Daniel Kuhn, **Alzheimer's Early Stages**, published by Hunter House, 1990, page 50

CHAPTER FIVE

1. Sharon Mahoe, **God's Words Of Life,** published by Zondervan Corp., 1997, page 82

2. Guy McKhann, M. D. and Marilyn Albert, Ph. D., **Keeping Your Brain Young,** published by John Wiley & Sons, Pub., 2002, page 7

3. Lawrence M. Tierney, Jr., Stephen J. McPhee, and Maxine A. Papadakis, **2001 Current Medical Diagnosis & Treatment,** published by Lange Medical Books/McGraw-Hill Pub., 2001, pages 620-621, 680, 1328, 700

4. VNAA, **Caregiver's Handbook, A Complete Guide To Home Health Care**, DK Publishing Inc., 1998, page 19, 20

CHAPTER SIX

1. Catherine Parker Anthony, R. N., B. A., and M. S. and Norma Jane Kolthoff, R. N., B. S., Ph. D., **Textbook Of Anatomy and Physiology**, published by C. V. Mosby Co., 1971, page 429

2. Patricia H. Rushford, **The Help, Hope, and Cope Book For Peopler With Aging Parents,** published by Fleming H. Revell Co., 1985, page 143, 144

CHAPTER SEVEN

1. E. C. McKenzie, **14,000 Quips and Quotes For Speakers, Writers, Editors, Preachers and Teachers,** published by Balker Book House, 1980, page 114

2. Lawrence M. Tierney, Jr., Stephen J. McPhee, and Maxine A. Papadakis, **2001 Current Medical Diagnosis and Treatment**, published by Lange Medical Books/McGraw-Hill Pub., 2001, page 1287, 103, 1082

CHAPTER EIGHT

1. Ron Dunn, **Will God Heal Me? Faith In The Midst Of Suffering**, published by Multnomah Books, 1997, page 195

2. Mary Kaplan and Stephanie B. Hoffman, **Behaviors In Dementia**, published by Health Professional Press, 1998, page 8, 158,

3. Lawrence M. Tierney, Jr., Stephen J. McPhee, and Maxine A. Papadakis, **2001 Current Medical Diagnosis and Treatment**, published by Lange Medical Books/McGrae-Hill Pub., 2001, pages 1074, 1092, 1241-1242

4. Philip Yancey, **Where Is God When It Hurts,** published by Zondervan Pub. House, 1977, page 83

5. Highline Homecare Services, **Hospice Notebook,** published by Highline Homecare Services, 1998, page 23-24

Printed in the United States
1231500001B/259-474